MIAMI

MIAMI

CONFESSIONS OF A CONFIDANTE

Regina Milbourne

AND YVONNE CAREY

ReganBooks
An Imprint of HarperCollins*Publishers*

Photographs on pages 7, 21, 77, 89, 109, 121, 179, and 197 by Eileen Soler; photographs on pages 1, 13, 33, 47, 63, 99, 135, 147, 167, and 215 by Yvonne Carey

HarperCollins books may be purchased for educational, business, or sales promotional use. For information please write: Special Markets Department, HarperCollins Publishers Inc., 10 East 53rd Street, New York, NY 10022.

FIRST EDITION

Designed by Kris Tobiassen

Printed on acid-free paper

Library of Congress Cataloging-in-Publication Data

Milbourne, Regina.
    Miami psychic : confessions of a confidante / Regina Milbourne and
Yvonne Carey.— 1st ed
        p. cm.
    ISBN 13: 978-0-06-084970-2 (alk. paper)
    ISBN 10: 0-06-084970-3 (alk. paper)
    1. Milbourne, Regina.   2. Psychics—Florida—Miami—Biography.   3.
Mediums—Florida—Miami—Biography.   I. Carey, Yvonne.   II. Title.

BF1283.M54A3 2006
133.8092—dc22
[B]
                                                                2005057569

06 07 08 09 10 WBC/RRD 10 9 8 7 6 5 4 3 2 1

FOR OUR LOVING CHILDREN: HILLARIE, SAM, AND
VINNIE MILBOURNE, AND ASA AND SPENCER CAREY,
WHO GIVE US A REASON TO STRIVE
FOR LIFE EVERLASTING.

AND FOR GOD,

FROM WHOM ALL GOOD THINGS COME.

Contents

Prologue

Hello. My name is Regina. I have a sixth grade education, I drive a Bentley, and I own a large, luxurious home in Miami, free and clear. I am a successful "boutique" psychic—that is, if making oneself available twenty-four hours a day to bloodcurdling clients is considered successful.

I never planned on being a psychic. I am still ambivalent. Because I believe I got the gift directly from God, I felt I had to do something with it. For more than fifteen years, I dedicated my life to helping *anyone* who needed help. Seduced by the power and the money it brought, I also took my share of the pie.

But now I am done.

With this book I will end my career as a master psychic. This book delves into case files and divulges the true stories of my work as a psychic with some of Miami's most controversial public figures. I have had many experiences with many clients. The stories I tell in this book are composites of those experiences. The names used are not the names of any of my clients, and the identifying details are not accurate as to any one of my clients. Each client had ample time to reconsider the amounts charged for work done. What has been important to me is to tell my story without revealing the identity of any one of my clients. By recounting these relationships to you, I will reveal that these are not typical counseling relationships. I tell these stories to bring to light what "average" psychic relationships are like. Yes, I can see future events. Yes, I have dealt with Santeria, voodoo, *mal occhio*, and curses. But what I really do is act as an unlicensed psychologist to people tangled in corruption of all sorts—corruption of this world and out of this world. Sometimes I help; sometimes I can only listen. Always, I carry the burden.

So, I open my book to you, not to breach any promises to my clients, as I never made any, but instead to come clean, to shock and entertain you, and hopefully, to begin to reform the huge, corrupt business of being a psychic.

ONE

Crystal Ballers

When people think of psychics, they think of the spooky, old gypsy woman at the carnival with the crystal ball on the table. That's not a psychic; that's entertainment.

People often ask me, "Are you the real deal?" or "How do I know you're a real psychic?"

Being a psychic is not something I learned from a book or just decided to be one day! After all, this is not something that you suddenly pick up as a new hobby or profession. Unfortunately, there are people out there that try to do so—and they give us true, gifted psychics a bad name.

This is a gift I received after a near-death experience when I was twelve. I then honed my gift at the Berkeley Psychic Institute to become a certified professional tarot and palm reader, astrologist, clairvoyant, and medium.

So what is a psychic? A psychic is simply someone who has the ability to see into the past and the future. A psychic can act as a healer, confidant, friend, miracle worker, counselor, or witch. She may supply a second opinion on physical ailments or whatever suits your needs.

A typical psychic reading may or may not involve tarot cards. Some, like myself, rely on meditation to reveal the truth. A typical psychic has spirit guides, visions, and vibrations to tell her she is on the right track. These guides are not evil; their job is to help. They can be anyone from an ancestor who has had the gift, to someone from a completely different cultural background, like an Indian guide who was once the tribal mystic. Everyone has spirit guides.

Good psychics will not make you ask questions. They will give you answers. Psychics have regular clients. Some return once a year, some every six months, and some (usually the very wealthy or disturbed) come weekly.

Switching from psychic to psychic is not recommended. If there is more than one psychic in your area and you are being counseled by both, you will mix their energies, visions, and power. As a result, not only will you get confused and lose your focus, but neither of their spells or meditations will work for you. Once you have a psychic with whom you're comfortable, who is doing specific work for you, stick with it. Be patient. Predictions are not always on your time schedule.

The charges for these services differ. The amount I charge reflects both how much the client can afford and the work involved. Some cases require volumes of supplies and take years to solve. Sometimes I inflate my fee if I'm reluctant to take the job. Some clients are demanding and insatiable. They may want love, money, or babies; the "feeling" put back in their vagina; or a "bailout" from jail.

In every case, I am fighting dark forces with my blood, body, soul, and mind. My life and karma are on the line. When I step up against the high Santero priests, or *Babalaos*, they can see me *telepathically*. They try to get inside my mind and dreams.

The client's commitment is invaluable. I need to see the person *invest* in *themselves*. I need to know that if I call them in the middle of the night and tell them to get up and go into prayer *right now*, they will do it. My clients need to value prayer as a way to restore faith in God. Faith in God is the operative determinant *because what I do won't mean a thing without God.*

Think of it this way: If you were a psychiatrist, how much would you charge to cradle a client through Christmas night? Or to speak to them every single night on the phone while that client questioned your credentials, demanded more attention, or even threatened your life? How many shrinks can say they know what their clients eat for breakfast, lunch, and dinner? How many can say they prayed for their client for two consecutive weeks?

Some people are in therapy for more than twenty years and never gain peace. Clients have told me their shrink diagnosed them with depression and told them the only way to fix things was through endless appointments and medication. But they'll come to me once, and I read for them. When I hit on something no one has ever told them before, you see the lightbulb go off in their heads, and they choose not to be victims anymore. I give them the confidence to feel like they can have peace. In many cases I'm their last hope.

TWO

American Gypsy

Even the word *gypsy* is misleading. People coined it based on the mistaken belief that all our descendants came from Egypt. My people came from Brooklyn, and we are Gypsies. We moved a lot, but not because we were aimless wanderers, with no plans for the future, like the Gypsies in the movies. We moved because my father, Marko, was an entrepreneur. He had many "businesses" with my Uncle Costi. It made my mother, Terena, extremely anxious.

I wasn't born psychic. Almost all the psychics I meet tell the same tale: they narrowly escaped death in a traumatic accident without so much as a scrape—like a plane crash that kills all the passengers but one. For me, it was drowning.

My family lived in a cramped, two-bedroom apartment at the time. I shared a room with two baby brothers. It was a jumble of polyester-flowered bedspreads and dirty socks. One summer, when I was twelve, my father found a way to take us to the shore. We were city kids. We never belonged to a pool and never learned to swim, but I always loved the water. My father borrowed Uncle Costi's Maverick to get us there. We drove for hours, my mother screeching at us to settle down, but we were all too excited. Finally the boys went to sleep, and I shut my eyes, concentrating, picturing myself playing in the ocean.

We pulled into the motel, and I spied a long, rectangular pool right in front of a strip of tiny motel rooms. I stared at it while I helped carry my little brothers inside. I tucked them in the bed they'd share with my mother and father. Then I made a nest for myself with a rolled-up bedspread on the floor. I was already dressed in my turquoise bathing suit.

The next morning I woke with a single thought—go to the pool! My mother kept saying, loudly, "Wait, Gina, we're not ready! You can't go right now. Ya hafta wait!" But I slipped out the door. A couple of sunbathers were already out on the deck. The water, sparkling like diamonds, hypnotized me. I had no idea that pools were deeper on one end than the other. I jumped in, but never touched the bottom. It was so cold. Instinctively, I tried push myself up out of the water, terrified because I couldn't breathe. Struggling, I begged God to get my mother. I guess, in the panic, I swallowed so much water it went into my lungs. Then, everything went black, and I was warm—no more terror.

I know this will sound totally cliché, but the reason you hear the same account about what happens when you nearly die is because this is *exactly* what happens. I found myself floating in the dark. I wanted to find someone to tell me where I was, and, as I drifted, I saw a beam of light. The closer I moved toward it, the more brilliant it became—like a beacon. I pushed forward, and then I heard a beautiful sound, almost like music, but it was voices. They kept repeating, *"Don't come in here."*

I said, "But I have to. I have to go to the light. I can't see."

I heard, *"You have to go back, Gina. There's something you have to do on Earth. You have to go back, Gina. You have to go back."*

The second I turned back, I opened my eyes, and I found myself in a hospital emergency room, somewhere in Ocean City, New Jersey. My father's face, inches from mine, was red and angry. Beads of sweat dripped from his curly, boot-shaped sideburns. He scolded me loudly: "How could you do this, Regina?! You could've died, girlie!! Your grandmother's gonna die when she hears!!"

"Stop it! You're makin' 'er cry!! You gonna put her into a trauma!" screamed my mother.

All I could think about were the voices and their message. All at once

I felt like someone else—someone more than Gina. About a month later, while we all slept, I heard the same beautiful voices, urging me to wake.

"Gina. Get out of the house. Get up, Gina. Get up. Get up, and get your family out of the house."

I thought I was dreaming, so I rolled over and snuggled into my pillow.

"Gina. Get out of the house. Get up, Gina. Get up. Get up, and get your family out of the house."

This time I saw a vision of my home consumed in flames, and I sprang out of bed. I grabbed the baby from his crib, pulled the covers off John and yanked him out of bed by his pajama collar. We rushed to our parents' room.

"Get up Daddy! Get up! The house is on fire! Get up!!! Please get up!"

He said, "Why? Is there someone in the house? Did you hear a noise? What's wrong, Gina?"

"We have to get out of the house, Daddy! Please get up; the house is on fire! Please get up!" I yelled, my voice growing higher and louder until I was nearly hysterical.

"Okay, okay, Gina, we'll get up! It's okay."

"Please Daddy! We have to get out!!"

I was still shrieking when finally I saw my father dial 911. I was unconcerned about the consequences should I have been wrong. In my heart there was no question. Slumped and dazed on the street curb in the damp morning air, we watched firefighters rush inside. Soon, one approached my father and told him there was a gas leak behind our stove. My father snapped his head toward me and searched my eyes, while my mother thanked the firefighters. He knew, all right. From that moment, he understood that I was not an ordinary little girl. My father never again doubted my visions or perceptions.

Throughout time immemorial, Gypsies have been mistreated for fortune-telling. In some places it's forbidden to even mention our existence because the the non-Gypsies believe we have some sort of alliance with the devil. But we don't. We *do believe* in one God. We just don't doubt that some people have visions, premonitions, or prophetic dreams. We never deny the power of a true God-given gift.

THREE

A Sign and Card Table

Noni was my mother's best friend. Noni was married to Costi. Costi was bad to Noni. He was always working but barely made any money, and she didn't even have any kids to comfort her. Consequently, Noni was always over at our house, with Mommy. She wore her long, black hair just like my mother, pulled back tightly in a large bun. She wore pantsuits like my mother, mostly cotton pique, some with gold piping. She even wore the same perfume as my mother—Tea Rose.

One morning, Noni came over very early, looking like she'd been crying all night. I answered the door.

"Hi Aunt Noni."

"Where's your mother, Gina? I gotta talk to her!"

"She's in the kitchen." Noni brushed past me, and I went back to watch the boys.

Johnny wanted some milk, so I went to the kitchen to get it for him. My mother and Noni were whispering over the sink. I stuck my head inside the fridge to get milk and tried not to eavesdrop.

"How do you know?" my mother asked.

"Oh, I know alright! I know, T! I wish I knew who it was! I swear to God I'm leaving that bastard this time! I bet Marko knows, don't he? I bet you know, too!"

As the words left her mouth, I saw a blonde in the doorway of a white townhouse, kissing my uncle good-bye. They were definitely in love, those

15

two. Then, I did the stupidest thing. Utterly ignorant of the potential backlash, I told the truth.

"It's the blonde in the white townhouse, Aunt Noni," I said.

My mother's eyebrows shot up. "What? What are you sayink girlie? 'Ush!! How do you know that? Tell me this minute—how you know?"

Then came the backhand on my lip with her wedding ring. "What do you know? Who told you? You don't know what you're sayink!" she screamed. A thin trickle of blood ran down my chin. Paralyzed, I just stared at Noni, who was observing my mother for clues about how much my mother knew. I suspect Noni got past the possibility that her best friend had been keeping Costi's secret and asked me quickly, "Gina, what blonde?"

Tears welling up in my eyes, I said, "Aunt Noni, I just saw a blonde lady kissing Uncle Costi in a doorway. I'm sorry. I'm so sorry Aunt Noni."

Dumbfounded, with her fingertips on her temples and mouth agape, my mother shook her head at me. It didn't matter. It's what I saw, and it was the *truth*.

"What's her name, Gina?" Noni asked.

"I don't know. I can ask. I'll try to ask," I offered sheepishly.

My mother had come back to life with a vengeance: "Who? Who you gonna ask, girlie? What kind of girl talks like that?" Wham! Another slap to the cheek.

"Leave her alone, T!" shouted Noni, simultaneously grabbing Mommy's arm. "Gina knows somethink, and she's the only one helpink me! Stop it! Lemme hear what she's got to say!"

"Gina, can you find out 'er name? Where she lives? And does he love 'er?" Noni asked me.

"I don't know how to ask them, but I will ask, Aunt Noni. I'm so sorry." I now knew better than to tell her he loved the lady passionately.

Then, effortlessly, I explained what happened back on vacation while I was supposedly "dead" for minutes. My mother rolled her eyes, sneered, and shook her head (she was very wary of the whole Gypsy fortune-telling thing and wanted to make sure I was telling the truth), but Aunt Noni wanted a reading.

"Gina, you hafta ask for me. Find out who this lady is, please Gina. It's grown-up stuff. You don't need to be afraid. You won't get punished anymore, right T?"

My back pressed against the refrigerator door.

"Gina, I don't want any more lies. I don't know what you've been listening to, but I don't want any lies in my house!" My mother meant it.

"I'm not lying, Mommy. I saw it in my head when Aunt Noni was talking to you." I walked back to the boys, forgetting the milk. I stopped in the bathroom, leaned over the sink, and checked out my lip. It stung a tiny bit. I begged whoever made the voices to tell me who this blonde was, but nothing came to me. I guess they felt that image was enough. As I wiped my chin with a little scrap of toilet paper, I contemplated my new powers of, I guessed, *intuition*? Were they something I could control, like on a TV show, where I'd seen a man lift a whole car, *by himself*, off his son who was trapped underneath? Or was I just being controlled? And why? What good came from telling Aunt Noni there was a blonde who lived in a white townhouse? Was the information supposed to help other people or me? Trying to understand how it all worked would later become my obsession.

The bottom line was that Noni needed information, and I was able to give it to her, like nobody else could. I was watching Uncle Costi and this blonde woman kiss, as if I were standing right across the street from them. I was like a private eye, but without even leaving my house. I also knew what I was watching was happening in the present time. As Noni was talking to my mother, Uncle Costi was kissing a blonde lady, somewhere across town. I felt it. I felt powerful.

I thought I was completely focused on the mystery of the vision when I saw the letters "B-A-R-B-A-R-A" flash like on a screen inside my head. Without hesitation I went straight to my mother and told her.

Hitting the back of her hand in her other palm, she said, "You're sure, Gina? I don't wanna get Noni crazy over nothing; this is very serious, Gina. You undahstand?"

"Yes, Mommy. I know."

"Okay, honey. Just so you know . . . I'm gonna tell her." With my mother, there's a lot of hazing before you become one of the girls.

Later that night, Noni came back and said, "Gina, come take a drive with me." Aunt Noni believed. She drove through a neighborhood I'd never seen. But I knew my way around it as if I'd been there before.

"Where are we going, Aunt Noni?" I asked.

"We're looking for somebody."

"Who?"

"We're looking for your Uncle Costi, Gina. We're looking for my no-good s-o-b husband."

"Turn left," I said. "Turn left right now."

"Whatever you say, Gina."

"Go down a little more. It's that one."

Aunt Noni gripped the steering wheel and slammed on dead brakes. My little body flipped off the seat and fell on the floorboards.

"Are you all right, Gina? Get up! Get up! Are you okay?"

I scrambled up as she dashed out of the vehicle and up to the switch-board and rang every single bell in the place, until someone let her in out of pity.

She called out, "C'mon Gina! Come with me! You need to confirm!"

We ran up a flight of steps, and when I saw a ceramic mezuzah, I felt sure that was the blonde woman's door.

"That's the one, Aunt Noni! What're you gonna do?"

"You sure Gina? I'm gonna kick her ass!"

She briskly knocked on the door, but no one answered. Then she pounded.

"Are you sure this is the one, Gina? You sure?"

"Yes! This is the one! I'm sure!"

"Are you positive?!

"Yes I'm sure!!" I said, gasping.

"'Cause I'm gonna kick 'er ass, Gina!! I'm gonna kick both their asses!! Up 'n down da street!!!"

But no one was there. Eventually she gave up and took me back home. I learned later she turned around and went right back to camp out in front of the building. She watched and waited until she saw Uncle Costi walk through the doorway with long-legged, blonde Barbara. They were coming back from dinner, arms linked together. Noni lost it. The way Uncle Costi tells the story now is completely different than what actually occurred that night. Half of his hair was torn clean off his head, and his upper lip was busted. Put it this way, my brothers and I awoke to the screams of a terrified man, pounding on our door for help in the middle of the night.

"I need a place to sleep!! She went crazy! She's trying to kill me!"

Noni left Costi, and Costi married Barbara, the *gaji* (non-Gypsy), one year later. They're still together. Shortly after, rumors spread that I was the town witch. Gypsies of all ages came to my house saying, "I need to speak to Gina! I need to speak to the little girl!" That ceramic mezuzah never left my mind. I spent the rest of the summer answering most of my relatives' questions, one by one, on love, lust, career, money, curses, angels, dear departed ones, and lost items. Spurred on by their praise, I became like a shaman in my little corner of the world, retreating from kids my age and reading books on divination.

Then school started again. Seventh grade was miserable. All my former girlfriends, from before I became "psychic," had boyfriends. Not me; news of the predictions and visions had leaked throughout my neighborhood and into the teen world. I was now known as a "freak." It suited me just fine because I preferred to spend all day with my grandma cooking. I cooked and watched my brothers, until someone came to me with their question. Then I would usher them into our bedroom, and say a little prayer, and ask the voices for guidance. Sometimes I got a vision; other times I didn't. That's why the kids decided I was a liar and a freak show, telling me their parents said I had the devil in me. Sometimes they would try to trick me.

The worst part was trying to concentrate at school. I could read books on divination well enough, but I couldn't focus on anything related to schoolwork, like math or social studies. I tried to read paragraphs but would end up either thinking about my ability or getting a vision. I got fed up. Also, my dreams were starting to get really detailed and vivid, so I wasn't getting much sleep. It was too much. Tired and inconsolable, I made my decision. I quit school and moved to Miami with my grandma.

For three years my grandma tested my skills by having me give free readings to strangers she stopped at the Aventura Mall. At seventeen, I set up a card table at Bayside Marketplace with a sign that read, *Psychic Readings $50.*

Bad Cop

Bayside was barely more than tourist shops on the waterfront back then, selling cheesy seashell-framed mirrors, Rasta hats with built-in dreadlocks, and flamingo refrigerator magnets. But it was an oasis in the middle of a homeless mecca—Beggars' Row.

All along the Biscayne Bay inlet that surrounded Bayside was a shanty village—pop-up tents and cardboard boxes, set up by destitute, expatriated Haitians and "snowbums" from up north. Beggars' Row is what kept the bankers and lawyers, who worked next to it downtown, from grumbling too much. It's what made me early for the bus every day, to get to my little card table. You could smell urine wafting inland from Beggar's Row on Biscayne Boulevard up to Second Avenue. But inside Bayside all you could smell were burgers and piña coladas. And it got a lot of traffic because cruise ships dumped their live load at the Port of Miami, just around the corner. Hundreds of sunburned, naive tourists, looking to kill a few hours "exploring Miami," had nowhere to go but Bayside. They came by the busload.

I set up right next to the Let's Make a Daiquiri stand and was making money hand over fist. At first I was open from 10:00 A.M. to 6:00 P.M., regular store hours, but I noticed that the party at Bayside started at four, when the salsa band played in the bandshell right in front of the daiquiri stand. So I adjusted my hours.

One evening in the summertime, when the sun was still a few minutes shy of setting, a stork-like he-woman paced up and down past my table, studying me and my clients. She had blonde, feathered hair and pasty skin, and her broad, square shoulders eclipsed her pointy breasts. Her blue chinos and polo shirt instantly made me feel she was a cop.

At first I feared she was going to harass me because of the misconception that all psychics are cons. I was also fearful she would arrest me because of the racist assumption that all Gypsies are thieves. At the time, I still dressed like a Gypsy—easily identifiable with a long, skirt, a long-sleeved shirt, pulled-back hair, and big gold earrings. Most of us can pass for Italian, Hispanic, or Greek, but the sure way of identifying Gypsies is through our speech. I, as most Gypsies do, love our dialect. Our favorite colloquialism is the word *youse,* as in "youse undahstand?" Or a very pronounced *k* when saying the *ing* ending, as in "the dinner in the oven is burnink." Real psychics are treated with respect among Gypsy elders. But you are expected to hold yourself to an almost divine standard and never show human weakness—a recipe for disaster. Not all psychics are Gypsies, and not all Gypsies are psychic. I just happen to be both.

The woman kept chewing on a red straw, looking at me with those piercing, blue eyes, while I read for an old Latino lady. The little old lady wanted to know if her son, who was getting a divorce, was OK in Washington, D.C. As I turned the third card for the old lady, I heard my guides say, *"Falling down."* As I continued to turn the cards for the old lady, inside my head I saw a vision of a brown man in a brown cowboy hat, getting bucked off a brown mechanical bull. Suddenly, it was gone, and I was looking down at the cards again. I knew this vision was not meant for the old Latino. I looked up and saw the blonde, right behind the little old lady, sweating and freaking out. She asked me, "Are you the real deal?"

I said, "Yes. I'll be with you as soon as I finish this reading."

"I'll pay you a thousand dollars to read me *right now.*"

The little old lady got angry and mumbled *"Puchika! Que desgraciado!"* (Gosh, what a jerk!) thinking this cop was a man. I told her to come back in two minutes, so I could finish with the old lady. I was able to finish it up quickly because I saw that her son was, in fact, gay and already with another man. As the old lady was getting up off the chair, in tears, the man-woman shoved her skinny ass on it and started telling me, without even waiting for the old lady to leave, that her name was Bobbie and she was being sexually harassed by the captain at the Dade County Narcotics Bureau.

I threw three cards. "I see you surrounded by drugs."

"I'm a narcotics officer."

"No. It shows drugs being sold," I said.

She looked more terrified than surprised. There was more to it than sexual harassment. She was one of this captain's narcotics officers. She said her house had just been broken into the day before. That morning, the captain, Ed Rohr, had called her in for a private meeting. When she went in, he locked the door behind her and said "I know you like it black, Bobbie. Why don't you give me a try? I'm more experienced than your rookie cop."

I said, "You're sleeping with another cop?"

"Yes."

"Look, let me throw the cards and see if this captain wants to sleep with you," I said.

The cards revealed he wasn't trying to seduce her. He was really coming on to her just to get her to admit to misconduct and something else. I told her the cards revealed the rookie she was sleeping with was married.

"What did you say to this captain?" I asked.

"I said nothing. Carrying on affairs with other married officers while on duty is not exactly the way to keep your job. Plus he wants more from me. Rohr is into something else, not sex. He wants information," Bobbie said.

"Okay, so you're stealing drugs at busts," I said.

"How do you know I'm stealing drugs? Where does it show that?" she said, freaking out again.

"Tell me more about what Rohr said," I instructed her.

"He said he'd gone to lunch with another cop—one of the rookies that went with me on many busts. At Monty's on the waterfront in Coconut Grove. The guy was mouthing off about one particular bust and how stupid the dealers were. They didn't hide the drugs, and they were just sitting there, out in the open on the dining room table when we came in. Well, Rohr questioned the cop. He said some of the drugs from the most recent bust right behind the Overtown Historic Village were missing. And the rookie said something like, 'Well, you know how sometimes a bag or two gets left behind, or somebody walks out with a bag or two for their own pleasure?' Then Rohr went to pay the check, and the rookie reached for it and said, 'No Captain, I'll get it.' Rohr wanted to know how a young cop could afford to pay for the food at Monty's on his meager salary. I'm the lead officer on the Overtown busts. Rohr wants a cut. So he tried to trap me and told me exactly how many bags were missing from the past thirty-seven busts, which is roughly, three months worth of busts."

"Well, the break-in at your house was definitely about drugs. He was looking for drugs or money. Listen to me. You need to stop whatever you're doing, Bobbie. It's no good. I saw it. You're going to fall down. My angel guides told me before you even sat down." I said.

"Look, Regina, I need protection; I heard people like you do stuff like 'protection spells' and whatnot. Can you do it?"

"I can. But I usually do it for women who get beat up by their husbands, or people going into the military, or children in the middle of custody battles, not for drug dealers."

"I'm a good cop, Regina. I swear. I'm not doing this for myself," she said, rubbing her eyebrow against the grain. "I'm supporting my old mother and my young son, who live in the Keys. I'm giving money to my lover and his family, and I'm trying to cash out my house so I can retire from this bullshit. Maybe my man will see how much I love him and leave his wife."

"He's not going to leave his wife, Bobbie. He doesn't love you. It's just about the money."

But I knew someone as homely as this poor woman wasn't going to give up. This was the only man who had touched her in many, many years. She really loved this married, rookie cop, even if he charged her for sex.

"Please Regina, please help me! I'm afraid Rohr's going to have me killed because he wants a cut so bad!" she said, grabbing my wrists so tight I thought she cut the circulation off.

"You gotta help me. We're talking hundreds of thousands *per bust*. I'll give you anything," she said.

"I don't know if I can help you because I can feel you won't stop this, Bobbie." I said pulling back my hands. "You want to keep stealing, Bobbie. It doesn't look good."

Bobbie dug in her pocket and threw down another thousand dollars. A man who had been blending daiquiris at the stand pulled the pitcher from the motor and yelled out, *"Who wants to try a delicious Miami Vice daiquiri! Step up! Nothing to it, but to do it!"*

"Look, this is just for now, and I'll give you whatever you ask. Just promise me you'll help me. I need someone to protect me."

"Miami Vice, people! Taste the good life! Live on the edge!" he yelled, raucously.

I admit, I was tired of eating leftover stew with my grandma and taking the bus down to Bayside, dragging my little card table and folding chair. And here was Bobbie: frightened, rich, and desperate.

"Taste it! Tell me it wasn't worth the wait!"

"Okay, how are you working it now?" I asked.

"I leave the bust and hide *my* bags in a special compartment under the seat in my cruiser. I made the pocket myself. It's big enough to hold fifty grams. Then I take the rest of the bags to Narco central. I dump the load and fill out paperwork. Then I take my drugs directly to my dealers waiting in Coconut Grove, on Hibiscus. When I get home, I hide the cash in Betty Crocker cake mix boxes in my kitchen cabinets. Nobody ever checks food containers."

"Why can't you just stop? Don't you have enough now? And besides, Rohr's watching. I feel Rohr is going to meet with your dealers."

"Gonna tempt you with another con-COCK-shun ladies . . . Anyone willing to try a Sex on South Beach?"

"Please Regina. You gotta protect me. I love Akwan. I never loved any man in my whole life, except this guy. I've gone through a lot for this man. I gave Akwan money, clothes, and toys for his kids. Furniture for his home."

"And then he has *sex* with you?"

"Yeah, but I think he would leave his wife if he sees I could give him more than she can," she said, smoothing her hair back.

"No, Bobbie. He will never leave her. He doesn't love you. I'm sorry, but I can't lie to you. And Rohr is aiming for bigger things, Bobbie. He doesn't want the money to spend. He wants to get out of the ghetto narcotics squad, Bobbie. He wants to be a politician. This is campaign funding. I see it."

Bobbie's jaw dropped. "How the hell do you know that?!"

"Because I'm the real deal, Bobbie. My gift came from God. Now I'm stuck giving advice to people like you who won't take it!"

"I'll give you anything you want! Please help me! I'm a white female in charge of five male cops! The white ones hate me for loving a black guy; the black ones hate me for screwing a rookie! They say to me 'chocolate must be sweetah than vanilla." They all hate me for being their boss—*because I'm white and a female!* I can't take it. Rohr takes every opportunity to fake like he's going to grab my crotch! I want to quit the force, but I need cash to start over. I have my mother down in the Keys to take care of. Every time I'm on a bust in Overtown, I see the little black babies crying, hungry, wearing nothing but a filthy diaper. These dealers in Overtown, they're not like the guys in the Grove, who sell to hippies and waiters. Overtown gangs step on the babies, Regina. God, I hate it! These guys take over an entire rundown apartment building and exploit the poorest people. They beat the shit out of little boys, kids like eight or nine, to make them sell their crack. Then they rape their sisters and mothers. I just walked in on one of these assholes last week. He'd forced a thirteen-year-old girl to smoke crack with him until she got addicted. Then when she'd come over asking if she could have some, he'd force her to have sex with him *and* any guys in the gang who wanted it. They have no heart! I beg you, Regina. Name a price. I need five more busts to get out and bring them down."

"A protection spell to protect an evil task requires lots of prayers and no guarantee. I would have to dedicate all my time to you. What you're asking is so deep, I don't know what to charge you! How can I put a price on my life?"

"Every time I see you I'll just bring a blank check . . ."

"I only take cash."

"And I can never meet you here at Bayside again. Too many officers around," she said throwing down another thousand dollars. "Can I come to your house?"

It was a doomed battle. I knew she was likely to die, but I didn't want to destroy her spirit. According to my feelings, I could protect her for at least four busts—enough to make at least eighty thousand dollars and get some of those bastards off the streets. So I strengthened my determination. I put a shield on her.

Every time I put a shield on someone, it requires three days meditation. I build an atmosphere of electrical energy around them. Prayers cling to the person according to the intensity of the emotion behind them to build this protective wall. I read that the CIA had put one around President Ford and Henry Kissinger so communist countries couldn't read their psychic thoughts. To eliminate the negative energies or anxiety surrounding her and to cleanse her aura, I cleansed her with oils and white roses for a week. I continued praying for seven days afterward, lighting a candle in my little prayer room in my grandma's apartment each day.

Bobbie got us secret cell phones so she could call me from anywhere at any time, for support or guidance. As she got stronger, she planned the busts flawlessly. She called me to pray with her each time before she went in and each time she got out. She even made the other cops join her in prayer for their mental and physical well-being. She delivered twenty thousand to me exactly twenty-four hours after each bust. One thing you could say for Bobbie, she never missed a payment. Three of the busts went smoothly. She put away some badass. Overtown drug lord named Dillis and pocketed more than a million in a month. Soon she forgot why she'd worried and became more obsessed with the rookie cop. One day, during our daily check-in phone calls before the fourth bust, I told her about the cowboy vision I had seen on the day I met her.

"Bobbie, this is it. You've got to stop. I'm getting visions of a brown man in a brown cowboy hat, getting bucked off a brown mechanical bull. It's your lover. His wife is about to find out."

"Okay, okay, Regina. This is it. No more after this, I promise. I swear I'll stop Akwan, too. I'm on the path, Reg. I mean it. This is the last bust and the last time I see him."

But she lied. Instead, two days later on Thanksgiving, she showed up at my house. She was a mess. I had to invite her in.

"I went to Akwan's house and gave him an ultimatum in front of his wife," she said. "She was screaming at me, in front of the kids. 'Are you fucking him? Are you fucking him? What do you want with us? You're nothing but an ugly white whore! Nobody wants you, you stupid whore. He don't want nothing to do with you no more!!'

"Akwan had to calm her down. I offered his wife $350,000 to pack up and leave. She won't leave him! Oh Regina, what am I going to do? Do you think he'll leave her? I miss him so much. He won't take money anymore. He told me I was a crazy bitch and he never wanted to see me again. Can you get rid of his wife, Regina? Please, I'll give you anything! Please help me! I'm so lonely!"

"I feel sorry for you, Bobbie. I really do. Deep down inside I know you have a good heart. But I cannot lie to you. He doesn't love you. It's not your destiny. I see you're doing a fifth bust, and the next bust is going to go awry," I said, handing her a tissue.

Cocking her head up, she confirmed my suspicions.

"How do you know I'm doing another one?"

"Look, Bobbie, I knew you weren't going to be able to stop. You're looking at death if you do it."

And my grandmother, who'd been cooking in the kitchen, came out, shuffling in her slippers and waving a wooden spoon.

"Gina don't go any further. You gotta stop calling her; you got what you paid for, and you be thankful to Almighty God! You test Him again, and He gonna test you. Praise God the Almighty for your health and sanity, what you got left, and move on."

As my grandma spoke to Bobbie, I got another vision. This time I saw a white bearded black man holding a deck of cards, and squeezing them. He squeezed them hard, into an inverted U, until they couldn't bend anymore. They didn't flip out of his hand; they just fell, one by one, to the grimy cement floor. And on the floor, there were three names.

Bobbie continued, "Someone's tipping off Rohr. He had someone break into the cruiser! They took a box of files on crack dealers and some photos. I have more files on these guys at my house; we've been watching them for months. This'll be the biggest bust we've ever done, and it's my last chance! I'll give you five hundred thousand dollars, Regina. Please protect me; please pray for me."

Confused, I tried to gain some time so I could evaluate the new visions in her case. "Bobbie, I see three names. They could be the ones who broke into your cruiser. Let me meditate on it, before you do anything. But I warn you, Bobbie, don't go on that bust!"

"Oh thank you!! Thank you, Regina!"

Anxiously, I prayed and meditated on the names for three days, and I saw a woman who worked on another unit, also being harassed by Rohr. I saw Rohr shoving her from behind, pressing his fingers into her shoulders and harshly hissing in her ears. I'm sure she was the one he had bullied into breaking into Bobbie's cruiser. The other two names were not coming up. I took a break and watched the evening news. There were reports on the tragic death of an officer killed in the line of duty in Coconut Grove, and his name sounded familiar.

I started to dial Bobbie's cell phone. Then I realized the dead officer's name was one of the three names I saw in my earlier vision. Bobbie's voicemail picked up. As I spoke, I saw her head, being tossed by some force, bleeding from the side, falling to the ground.

I said, "Bobbie? The person who broke into your cruiser is a woman. She's youngish, with red hair. And Bobbie . . . please don't go to the bust! Please promise me you won't go! Call me back and promise me you won't go on that bust!! I have to tell you something! Call me back immediately!"

Bobbie never called back.

FIVE

Container

began to feel vulnerable down at Bayside. It was too close to the Miami Bureau of Narcotics offices located downtown. I felt people were keeping an eye on me, especially the cops who patrolled Bayside.

Three months went by. One afternoon, a huge, macho Cuban cop came up to my stand. His forearms were covered in a thick blanket of curly, black hair. Little tufts poked out here and there from his shirt collar. Playing it cool, he swaggered up to my stand. He smelled like Drakkar cologne.

"Can you do me a reading about a frien' o' mine who's missing?"

I didn't even wait to hear who his friend was. I knew he meant Bobbie.

"I don't do missing persons," I lied.

"I heard you're the real deal," he said, grinning.

"Nope. I just do love connections and career forecasts, and I'm about to close, so thanks for stopping by and have a good evening, officer," I said, putting the cards away and folding my chair. "Sorry."

He stood up and looked frustrated, but he didn't have a thing to say to keep me.

I made my way to the bus stop and stared straight ahead. Sometimes, my best visions came while I was waiting for the bus. I was looking for a direction—a sign. The Port was good money, but things were getting slow. There were more tourists not wanting to spend, more families, and less drinking, with increased police presence. It was becoming increasingly clear I needed to move on. I prayed and prayed while I lingered. I saw shifting, aching, tired, platform-heeled feet. Then I heard sharp high heels clicking on the pavement behind me, click-click-click-click-click-click-click-click-click, getting sharper and louder. I turned to see who or what, but no one was there. Click-Click-Click-Click-Click-Click-Click-Click. In a vision I saw two beautiful ankles attached to two well-groomed feet, balancing atop stacked, knife-edged wooden wedges.

"Not in Bayside," I thought to myself, boarding the bus.

More months went by at Bayside, until one night I encountered an extremely wealthy middle-aged lady, who was on her way downtown to meet her husband for dinner. Her hands, neck, and ears were covered in gold and diamonds. Her reading was long and boring, as most of them are. Giving a boring reading is a mortal sin for a psychic. So, not infrequently, I undertake overly theatrical presentations with weak tricks for no payoff. Yet, this time I got a callback. It seemed her husband owned a store in the Jeweler's Exchange in what's now known as Aventura. She was going to a "boutique party" to get rid of some of his unwanted stock—flawed diamonds, gold, and some stones. I was invited to give readings "because I was so good." So after my shift that night, I waved good-bye to Bayside in gusty, rain-drenched winds.

They set me up in a softly lit corner of a large family room. To my left was a lady selling knock-off Louis Vuitton, Prada, and other brands—all bootleg. She introduced herself to me after my first client got up. Her name was Gela Gottex.

I could tell by the accent that she was Israeli. In her mid-forties, she was skinny, dark, and curly haired—fried and dyed.

"Are you really psychic? Do you like my bags? Are you gonna buy? Take the Fendi. I'll give you a great deal! You like Prada? I can trade a bag for a reading. My husband gets the Prada and Chanel next week from the Port of Miami. Or you can pay me now, and I'll mail it to you. Who do you work with, angels or demons?"

"Yes. Yes. No. No, thanks. No, I like the LV. Okay. Angels." I said grinning. My mind has always been as sharp as a whetted knife, keen and hungry.

"Oh! Angels. You're so lucky! But how do you know? How do you know for sure?"

"An angel is a pure spirit created by God. They are spiritual beings who reside in heaven, employed by God. The word *angel* comes from the Greek word *angelos*, which means 'messenger.' In the Old Testament, the Hebrew word for angel is *malak* and also means 'messenger.'" I explained, smoothing my paisley tablecloth.

"Yeah, yeah, but how do you know that what is guiding you is an angel?"

"Because they saved my life and my family's life," I said, exasperated.

"Hmm . . . and you're sure they're not just some demons trying to trick you into thinking that they're angels?" she asked, shoving change into the hand of a customer.

Before I could answer, a Colombian lady came and asked for a reading. As I read, Gela was making two, three, four deals at a time. The Colombian lady asked if I could I do a protection spell on her because her ex-husband was threatening to slit her throat. Gela's eyes fixed on me.

I said, "Come see me tomorrow. I can't do a protection spell right here on this spot, at this time."

While the Colombian lady recovered from the thought of having to spend one more night in fear of her life, Gela shouted over, "What do you see for me?"

"I don't give free samples." I said, wrapping my client's sweater around her shoulders. I wondered if Gela's timing in her professional life was as bad as her timing in her personal life.

"You want a purse? I can trade you a Fendi, or look, I have Gucci, Louis Vuitton, I have everything. I'll trade you for a reading."

"Fine."

Gela picked up the glass jar where she kept her cash, walked around her table, picked out the largest LV tote, and sat down in my client chair.

"This is the best one. These handles won't break," she said.

"So what do you want to know?"

"Is there anything gonna happen to me? Bad? I think some people are trying to kill me."

"Why do you think that?" I asked, starting to shuffle the cards.

"Forget it. I'm not giving any information up. You tell me what you see in the cards," oblivious to the words that she'd uttered that had given her away.

I threw down three swords.

"Doesn't look good." I said, but the reality was I became again distracted by the dissonant clicking of stacked heels against a concrete sidewalk inside my head.

"What? What? Tell me what's so bad!"

"Gela," I said, throwing five more cards down, "I think you're right. This is not symbolic death," I said, pointing at the death card. "This is not change. I feel this is a warning."

"*I knew it!!*"

"You have something. You stole something. You're carrying something. Something very bad," I said.

Gela's eyes stretched wide with dread. I would have laughed at her expression if the truth weren't on the table. She leaned in and whispered, "Last month, a man followed me out of a restaurant near my house to my car, and if I hadn't got the keys in fast, I swear he would have killed me."

After throwing the rest of the deck, it was revealed she was in grave danger.

"You gotta help me with a protection spell. You gotta keep me alive. My husband lost his business. We had a bad partner, and he stole everything and then sued us. My children need me, and my husband hasn't worked in months. I'm all we got!" she said.

I explained to Gela that I could not do a protection spell on the spot. There were many ways of performing a protection spell.

"I'll give you any amount of money you want! I need a protection spell! How long does it stay on for? A few months? How much do I have to pay for extended coverage? I need protection for a year, continuously. I need the best you got. But it better work! Please help me!"

I told Gela that the best type required me to fast for days in a sweat lodge, which is a little stone or skin teepee, with coals burning. I would use the one I trust in Sedona. Inside, I roll a prayer chain. That's a blessed, sacred chain made from tobacco and prayers (sometimes up to five hundred of them). I keep rolling the long yards of linen or paper filled with prayers as I loudly chant my client's name. Then I need one hundred and twenty Tibetan bowls: one for every year of her life and one for every day that I worked for her. I meditate for three days minimum. I couldn't go in during my menstrual cycle because I had to be purified. Once pure, after fasting, meditating, and rolling, I could make full contact with the spirits. Spirits continue to speak to me for five days by automatic writing. This costs one hundred and fifty thousand dollars. I had to turn myself into a shaman, and the only way I can get that magnificent power to come forward is to leave myself. I had to free myself from electricity, from food, everything. A sneeze or a cough would destroy everything and could put the client in danger. This kind of protection spell lasts up to three years. Slack-jawed, Gela was stunned.

Then I explained another kind of protection spell. It involved a cleansing. I put the person inside a bath or box, with white rose petals and holy water. I light two white candles. Then, I'd take an object, like a doll or a toy, which represents the person or thing feared. I bind up the object with black ribbon and say "I bind you from doing any type of harm to this person." Then I use wax paper and a special tool that looks like a toothpick and write the person's name down, with a special blessed ink and a special prayer for protection, peace, and success. I bind up the person's paper and prayer with a white ribbon. Then I say, "You cannot come close to her."

Lastly, I would have to take all of this to a sacred place and bury it for seven days under a waxing moon until the spell is conjured, or it wouldn't work. That's the generic, cheap one, for fifteen thousand dollars, but I needed to know the name of the person from whom the client needed to be protected.

"I'll the take the one for fifteen thousand."

"You need a name."

"Do it! Bind everyone. That's the one I want!"

"I'll see what I can do." I said.

It's a comedy-adventure in development and will when clients come to me for protection. Rarely is anyone's own life worth more than a Dodge Durango.

She arrived at my house the next evening, in her Sebring convertible, dressed in a black bejeweled pantsuit and one of her fake Chanel bags. Her style was a combination of QVC and Second Hand Rose, a consignment shop over on the Dixie Highway.

"Thank you for working so quickly, Regina. Someone followed me again last night from the house."

In my little office, I had the necessary items for her protection: white candles lit, prayers written in blessed ink, black ribbon, white ribbon, and white roses. She brought a picture cut out from a magazine of a man in a trench coat, representing the person she thought was trying to kill her.

Already, we were batting a thousand.

I asked her to close her eyes and focus. I pulled the petals off the roses and scattered them inside an old cardboard packing box, left over from my move from New York. I wrote her name and the names of her children on the box. I poured holy water over the rose petals. Then I asked Gela to step inside the old box and to sit down the best she could, without breaking it. I smoothed down her fried hair. I placed my palm on the top of her head and began.

"Yea, though I walk through the valley of the shadow of death, I fear not . . ." I continued with many a ceremonial and flowery phrase. The clients love that, but I was competing with heels click-clacking in my head.

"Gela," I said, "What's happened between the time you started selling bags and the night at the boutique party?"

"A lot of things. Finish up the protection. I can't go home without this!"

40

"No, Gela, I'm sorry, but you have to tell me what has happened, in detail. And slowly," I said, putting the prayers down.

So Gela began telling me that her husband once owned an import company based in Doral, in the western Miami area. The company imported textiles from the Middle East. He lost the import company to his partner over an alleged contractual dispute. The partner said her husband was in breach and threatened to sue them for everything they had. Instead of going to court over it, her husband, for some reason, chose to leave it alone and became unemployed. They had very little savings and no education.

One night, her husband said he knew someone who wanted to sell replica designer bags made in Israel in the United States through a sales representative. Gela was thrilled at first because she thought her husband would open up a trendy boutique. Instead, he had her sell them through word of mouth, out of the back of the car, and at boutique parties. She relented when she found out that no overhead resulted in more cash for the family.

Back then, Louis Vuitton was not as popular and considered out of reach for some people. Her husband set up a "boutique party" in a friend's home in North Miami, with a massive crowd of label-starved Jewish-American princesses willing to buy bootlegs to satisfy their need to save money and keep up with the Joneses.

A Junoesque Lebanese woman named Yolla became her best customer, buying almost all of Gela's stock at one time. Gela made a killing because this woman never haggled and paid only in cash.

Though Gela was the one raking in the dough, she had to give all the cash to her husband. She never got to spend any of it on the kids or herself. Somehow, the house and bills were paid—she assumed by her husband—and the kids simply did without extras. However, Gela didn't mind the crunch because her husband said they were saving to retire. Week after week, Gela would work a boutique party somewhere in Miami. And week after week, Yolla would buy out all but two or three bags. Where Yolla went with them, Gela didn't care, as long as the woman paid.

There was one tiny glitch. Yolla rubbed Gela the wrong way so badly, it pissed her off. By the tenth week, Gela had had enough.

"She's a bitch, Regina," she growled, teeth clenched, gripping the sides of the cardboard box.

"God help me, she's a no-class bitch orderin' me around. She says, 'Gela, bag those purses and put them in my trunk.' Handin' me the keys to her car like I'm some kind of valet! She thinks just 'cause she's got more money than God, she can come to my table and treat me like dirt in front of all them people at the purse party. She's got another thing coming to her. She don't know how much I had! I don't come from nowheres. She don't know my people! And I especially hate the way she walks in them heels she always wears—them high-stacked whore heels, thump-thump-thumpin' across the tile floor at the houses! Here comes the queen, oh! Make way for Queen Yolla!" Gela hissed.

"So I told her to beat it! I don't need her money. I got a lot of other customers!"

For two weeks, Gela had not sold to Yolla and soon after, someone started following her.

"Gela," I said, "You need to figure out why Yolla needs so many purses and why she wants to buy them from *you*. I heard her high heels getting louder as I was praying over you, and she's not a random customer who loves bootleg designer bags."

The story Gela told me about her business and Yolla quelled the noises in my head. The spirit guides got their message through, and I was able to complete the protection spell.

"I'm going to meditate on this, and after I'm done, we can decide what else you need," I said.

"And it's guaranteed?"

"Umm-hmm."

After I meditated the next day, I saw a lot of drugs. Drugs all around Gela, all around Yolla. I mean the really bad stuff: heroin.

I called Gela and said, "You need to call some of your clients and ask around. See if any of them have had any problems with drugs."

"I see them only once, twice a month, at best. I don't know anything else about them, other than they always come to my house to pick up their bags."

"Why does Yolla need so many bags?" I asked.

"She says her friends like the bags so much that they're picking up a bag or two for so and so, or they're picking up a new style for their niece," Gela said.

"Look, I'm not going to lie to you. I feel your life is in danger. I see drugs all around you. My guides are telling me the handbags and the drugs are connected. I heard Yolla's heels clicking on the pavement. The cards revealed someone was out to kill you."

"What are you saying—that I'm dealing drugs? It is perfectly legal to sell a replica purse. I am an importer of women's fashion handbags! It's all down on paper! It's all legal!"

"Gela," I responded, now genuinely upset, "You come to me for help. You come to me for advice, but you don't want to listen to what I say. You're not accepting what I'm seeing."

Suddenly her tone changed, and I felt her heart speaking to me. "Please help me Regina! How can I sell the bags if they're gonna be my death? I have to sell them, or my husband threatens me. It's the only form of income we got, Regina! Where do you think the money I pay you comes from? You ask your 'angels' to put the puzzle together for you, Regina! Do it for me now! You gotta help me!!"

I sighed, "That's fine, Gela. Just make sure you come by and pay me five thousand tomorrow, for all my meditations." I hung up. This is typical of people who seek my help and protection. When things don't happen the way in which they think they deserve or fast enough for them, they become short-tempered and nervous. By trying to control exterior factors, they sacrifice their peace of mind.

They seek me out, and though they have the money, they don't want to part with it. That's why I work so hard in meditation to give them something bona fide so they trust me. I have to go beyond normal psychic vision and pull something out of their life, so they'll trust me. After that, if they don't trust me, there's nothing I can do for them.

When Gela came to give me my money, she was very upset.

"Regina, I think you should help me check the next shipment at the Port when it comes in. I need you to check it."

"I don't do that kind of thing, Gela. I'm not a detective. I'm a psychic. I meditate and have spirit guides and see beyond the range of normal human vision. I do not physically hunt for clues. But because I can see you're in need of support, I'll do it. I'm gonna have to charge you a flat ten thousand dollars," I said, bluntly.

In retrospect, I should have charged a helluva lot more.

As we drove down to the Port, I thought, "God, I shouldn't be with her. What if someone involved with the drugs has followed her?"

I didn't want anyone from the boutique parties to find out that I associated with her, either, because this sort of thing gets around, and it never turns out good for me. When a problem arises and there's a psychic involved, the first person to be blamed is always the psychic. When the problem involves drugs, well, let's put it this way: There's no witness protection program tough enough to safeguard a psychic. Drugs and psychics have always gone hand in hand. Colombian drug czars and their Santeros. Only czars need protection; the Santero provides it or says he will provide it. But if the drug czar goes down, every man falls, including the psychic. The cops think the psychic was privy to every last detail of the smuggler's life. The traffickers think the psychic either tipped the cops off or just plain did not provide protection. In either case, neither the cops nor the traffickers let the psychic go. And the psychic ends up dead. Period.

I made Gela stop at the Department of Motor Vehicles in Miami Beach. A Cuban named Sharkey worked there. He supplied the whole of Miami with fake IDs. Mind you, this was prior to 9/11, when they were easy to get.

How he wormed his way into the DMV is another chapter completely. Sharkey is a real charmer—clever and gorgeous. After he supplied himself with his first fake ID, he got the job at the DMV and turned a $10-an-hour job into a $3.5 million-a-year career. Yes, he made that much. Who do you think began supplying the Arabs with IDs?

My plan was to get another ID to show customs, should I need to fly back into the States at a later date. So I stood in line until I could get Sharkey's attention. He was sweet on me. Within a few minutes, he came over to me.

"Gina, ahhh. Gina, you miss me, Gina?"

"Not if you were the last man standing, Sharkey. I need something from you," I whispered, smiling coyly.

"What name?" he asked.

"Maria Andrade," I answered.

"You don't look like a Maria. You still living with your grandmother?" he said as he began peeling the plastic off a card.

"Yes. Don't get my bad side this time, Sharkey." I teased.

"Regina, you don't have one. A bad side, that is, baby. I'd like a picture of your *back*-side. I would blow it up and hang it on my wall," he grinned. "When you gonna go out wit' me?"

"When pigs fly, Sharkey. Ready?" I said flipping my hair back and smiling for the photo.

"Seriously, you need to settle down sometime, baby."

"True. But a man like you would make me very needy."

In a few minutes, the ID was done, and Maria Andrade left the building, ready for the Port of Miami.

There was little activity at the Port that day as Gela and I pulled into the lot. The breeze smelled of fresh seafoam, effervescent and tingly. She parked her Sebring miles away from the warehouse. A barge transferring a black and yellow container held the only people, it seemed. I stepped out of the car and caught sight of old Bayside, miles and miles away from where I was now operating. I swung around to follow Gela, who was already halfway up the road. After a few minutes of appeasing the old Puerto Rican guard, we found her container, just in. She presented a pass and opened the container. I slipped through some packing and felt the box. We lugged it out. Gela pulled out an Exacto knife and expertly slit the lining in the seam. In seconds, I had one purse out of the box, lining slit to the zipper, exposing little bags of drugs.

We checked a few more, put everything back inside the box, put the box in the container, and shut the container. We thanked the guard pro-fusely with a few hundreds.

"So where are the kids?" I asked Gela as we sped off.

"Waiting for me at Miami International Airport. I'm dropping you at the Omni. Catch a cab back up North."

"Dump the car on your way," I warned her.

"Gina, don't worry. And thank you for all your help!!"

We estimated there was four hundred thousand dollars worth of counterfeit Louis Vuitton and Chanel handbags—and more than seven million of narcotics inside the linings in that shipment alone.

Gela and the kids would have to keep running the rest of their lives, and I needed to move my grandma and me—just as soon as I got home.

SIX

Sick Bastard

I went undercover.

Translated, that meant no boutique parties, no card table at a trendy mall, and no live readings.

It meant a small ad in a local New Age newspaper, doing ten three-hundred dollar readings over the phone a day.

In this great country of ours, there is nothing that can keep any one culture down if it is determined to grab the "brass ring" of a better life. So, I moved back to North Miami to pursue the American Gypsy Dream. There are some things worth fighting for, even if you lose.

I married a Gypsy man named Romy, whose family bought me for twenty-five thousand dollars, in accordance with Gypsy tradition. The price was higher than usual because I come from one of the better Rom tribes. I liked him well enough, and he was very supportive of my abilities.

Romy and I bought a 1930s Spanish-style fixer-upper that needed a lot of work. I sunk two hundred thousand dollars into it and blew it out. I added a Mediterranean pool and Jacuzzi, with tiles imported from Florence, marble floors from Spain, and hardwood moldings from Brazil. The slickest thing about Miami is that you can deck out your house with things from all over the world at any time, cheaply and swiftly.

While many *gaje* have an image of Gypsies being beggars and thieves, migrating around in raggle-taggle bands, Miami Gypsy houses and of course their cars, have a different tale to tell. Many of us have done quite well because of our versatility. I loved the idea of finally having a show-place in which to entertain my fellow Gypsies—especially those who thought I was psychotic, not psychic.

After months of laying low, I was determined to have a proper Miami house warming to usher in the mastery of my game. I called in caterers from Chef Allen's, the hip nouvelle cuisine restaurant, and ordered all the latest culinary creations, from starfruit to sea bass. My house was decked with seven thousand dollars worth of hothouse flowers and security cameras.

Although Gypsy women are confined to long skirts because exposing the lower body is deemed impure, I wore a short sundress. My sundress cost four thousand dollars. I was only twenty-three.

I invited every Gypsy I knew and even flew some in from New York. I played it like a real American Gypsy princess. People took notice all right. The florist Bennett Candy, who overcharged me for orchids that barely lasted through dinner, noticed.

"We're bringing in the last of the arrangements, Ms. Regina. Where would you like them?" he asked earlier that afternoon, scanning me with his eyes.

"Just make sure all the tables have flowers, and don't put the same type of arrangements next to each other," I said.

"It's been a great pleasure working with you, Ms. Regina," he gushed. "You have impeccable taste. May I ask where you acquired such exquisite taste in decorating?"

I was busy and did not have time to chat, especially with the weasely Bennett Candy. The frail, excitable, Armani Exchange–clad florist had the reputation of being a sponge. I'd hired him through a referral from a client, who had great taste but poor judgment. I lay down the hammer.

"Everything I have and everything I am is owed to God."

"Oh, I see. Well, may God continue to bless you, and thank you." He whimpered and slunk away.

But Bennett Candy was not the kind of man who let things go. If he saw someone throwing a lot of money around, he would find out where it came from—and then he'd suck the life out of that person. If you were a drug czar, he'd weasel you for dope. If you were a rock star, he'd harass you for backstage passes. If you were a psychic. . . .

One day, Bennett called and asked if an ad he'd seen in a prominent New Age newspaper was mine. He begged me for a reading, so I complied. I told him his male partner of thirty years was cheating on him with a woman. He said he felt dizzy and hung up.

Soon after, I received many calls for my services—all referred by Bennett Candy. The money was great, but the clients were a bit psychoneurotic, I thought. Then along came George.

"Hi! My name's George. I heard about you from a friend. He said you're really good. I'd like one of your sessions. Do you take credit cards?"

I told him I only took cash and that he could come see me in my office on the beach.

"I can't. It's complicated. People might recognize me. Can I get a phone session?"

"Okay, then. You have to send me three hundred dollars and a metal object you've had on your person for a while—a penny, a dime, a key chain, something you've kept in you pocket. Oh, and a photograph." I felt the darkness right away.

He said, "Do you feel anything? From me?"

"I know you need help."

I received a small FedEx package the very next morning. The cash was inside a greeting card, along with a photograph. He was standing next to his dad in a black Member's Only jacket and khakis. I didn't think anything more about it.

George seemed to have eyestrain in the photo. He had dark curly hair, squinty brown eyes, and olive skin. Except for an earring, he appeared conventional. But I knew instantly, through my guides, that he was not. I opened the tarot and saw a lot of really big issues.

I called him up and said, "I want to do your reading, now. I see you work in the entertainment field because you love the attention. Even as a child you demanded a lot of attention. You enjoy all kinds of weather. You've made a name for yourself, predicting things. Like me, George. And you've focused heavily on your career. Should I know you George?"

He chuckled.

"I see your father was extremely abusive to you, emotionally, verbally, and physically, and still is. His cards are coming up all around you, and you are the central figure in this spread. Your mother wishes you were married. Your father makes no bones about wanting you to be absolutely heterosexual. Are you gay, George?"

"Yes," he answered quietly.

"George, I see you have no partner, no children, nor the slightest desire to have any. But you have the inclination to beat yourself up over not having that desire. Are you afraid of children, George?"

I heard him quietly sobbing.

George then told me that whenever he had called his father for advice in the past, his father would say he'd never make it alone and that he was a failure. But to me, his mother seemed weirder. He said she'd call him and tell him when to clean his room, when to do his laundry, and how to prepare his food. He also had programs he'd watch with his mother while they were on the phone together. Their programs came on at special times. He wasn't allowed to talk at that time because she would get upset. George also said he heard voices and couldn't sleep, though he was tired all the time. Finally, George said, "Regina, I can't get an erection the . . . the normal way. No matter what I try to do. I haven't been able to in about ten years. But I try to find ways to, you know, get off."

"I see you have all these issues, George. And you say you hear voices, you can't sleep, you can't get an erection, your mother is codependent on you, and you haven't had sex in ten years. George, there comes a point in your life when you know you're being abused and you have to stop it— some way, somehow," I said.

Now I looked at George's picture again and wondered which, out of all of these, was the main problem in his life.

"I'm going to meditate on this. There are many factors here and a terrible darkness. Let me call you back tomorrow."

That afternoon, as I went into meditation, I saw the first trial. My guides told me his paternal grandmother and all of her descendants were cursed by *mal occhio*—the evil eye. *Mal occhio*, cast on someone by a jealous person, can give you migraines, watery eyes, eyestrain, dull thinking, lack of energy, fatigue, an overall uncomfortable feeling. I felt a dark spell over the whole family, but it came through the father's mother. George exhibited most of the symptoms.

I asked George about it the next day, and he said the family had heard they had *mal occhio,* but didn't take it seriously.

I said to him, "You're a grown man, and you can't get an erection. Your dad is a tyrant; your mother is codependent. Do you think this is normal? I'm going to figure this out and clean it up, George. But after I clean it up, we need to talk. By then, hopefully, we'll have the answer to your problems."

Mal occhio removal can be as simple as asking God's forgiveness through special prayers for several weeks while bathing in holy water or as hard as flying back to the site of the *mal occhio*'s origin and getting spat on by the descendants of the one who cast the evil eye on you. It's like a stain. This one had been on them for generations. Neither method was going to come cheap. George sent me a FedEx package with ten thousand dollars in cash in a greeting card to get started. I had a nickname for his FedEx packages—the Hallmark watermark.

Three more weeks went by, and I sent him some holy water, spat on by three men jilted by women, in which to bathe. Then after two months, I had the first breakthrough. Some of his symptoms—the eyestrain and the sleeplessness—disappeared. I meditated some more, and I saw the second trial—very dirty, very disgusting porn. My guides said he had to purify himself completely.

I called his cell immediately, "George, George! Is this George?"

"It's me, Regina."

"George, oh my God, I know what it is! You have porno tapes under your bed. George, what kind of porn is this?"

"With men."

"George, have you been going to see prostitutes?"

"Yes."

"These are not regular prostitutes are they?"

"No."

"George, you wash your hands sixty times a day. You take at least four showers a day, sometimes more. How can you be with a prostitute?"

"I don't let them touch me."

George said he would get two young guys, maybe eighteen years old, and watch them have sex with each other.

"George, do you get an erection when you watch this?"

"It appeases me."

I said, "George, I don't understand."

He said, "I don't understand either. I need help. I feel like it's wrong, but I'm compelled." He told me he watched the porno tapes at least three times a week with some young guys dressed as women. Sometimes George dressed in women's clothes, too.

I said, "George, the guides are telling me that what you do is wrong and immoral. It has to stop."

He begged me not to be upset with him.

I said, "I really want to try to help you. I know I was given this ability for a reason. But you must understand, George, your behavior has to stop."

The next day I got a FedEx envelope that contained a long list of things he couldn't control that ranged from blinking uncontrollably to suicidal thoughts. George also wrote that he kept hearing *Goodbye Cruel World* by James Darren, an old fifties song, playing like a recording over and over and over in his head. While I was reading this list, the phone rang, and I knew it was him.

"Did you get my list, Angel?" Angel was his nickname for me.

"Yes I did, George, but tell me—I feel like someone is listening to our conversations. My guides tell me someone is listening to our conversations."

"No! Nobody, Angel. It's just me."

I said, "Are you sure about that?"

"Yes, Angel—but I do tape record all our conversations."

I told him that was illegal.

"I listen to the tapes because they comfort me. Finally someone understands me so much that I can tell them my deepest darkest secrets. I need confirmation all the time, and when you tell me I'm not meant to be watching these men and that I'm not meant to be sick, you comfort me."

I told him that I wouldn't allow it and that he was to destroy the tapes.

He said, "But if you ever drop me, I have something to remember you by."

"George! What do you mean by 'drop you?' I am a psychic, not your girlfriend. When we're done, that's it. We are not in this for a long-lasting relationship."

"Well, my biggest fear is that one day I'll call your number and it will be disconnected. I don't have a lot in this world, and your friendship is everything!"

I heard soft sobbing on the phone.

"George, I am a friendly person, but you cannot think our relationship is anything more than professional. You do have more in this world than me. You have a successful career! You have yourself! You have the hope to get better. Have you been meditating?" I asked.

"Yes, and it makes me feel better, but I had some dreams I'm curious about. I have to write them down and send to them to you."

I said, "Fine, fine. Rule number one for healing: When you need something from God, you have to ask forgiveness and clear your soul of any heaviness or grudge of any kind that causes guilt or weight."

"Angel, I'm going to send pictures of my house and letters filled with all my dreams."

"George. Stay focused. I'm working on your case, nothing more." He hung up.

I did long-distance Reiki on him from his photo for nearly six more months, purifying, clearing, and breaking up negative things going in and out of his head. Reiki is a natural healing method thousands of years old that heals on all levels: physical, emotional, mental, and spiritual. Reiki summons healing energy from a higher power, or what I call heaven. I also used pyramids to keep him balanced. Usually a pyramid is used to draw energy from the higher power. Pyramids are very powerful. It is believed that their four corners represent peace, vitality, strength, and awareness. Some people believe they represent good fortune, wealth, health, and prosperity. You can even write your prayers or wishes underneath the pyramid. I channeled his guides to strengthen him. I prayed constantly for his release from despair and lit special candles.

Every day the FedEx man would come with another package from George. I'd sign for it, tear it open, take out the Hallmark card with the money, and toss the rest aside. I thought I knew all I had to know about George. I didn't feel the need to look at more pictures or more lists. I trusted his boyish nature. All I needed was the cash for my time, supplies, and phone bills. Just when I felt it was too much work for me, that I couldn't do any more for him—I mean at that instant—he'd call me and say things were much better.

"I feel great! The music in my head has stopped, and I feel great!" George would say.

"Wonderful!"

"But I still have the urge to watch young men, Regina, and I've come to find that women's menstruation turns me on. Is this normal?"

Floored, I hung up, and meditated more on his case to ask my guides where this thing was headed. Two hours later he called me and said he was sitting in Salvador Park, on a bench watching two little boys, gaping at their crotches and getting hard.

"I'm hard as a rock, Angel. You know it's the evil eye."

George was getting swept away by his *own* lunatic flow, in smaller and smaller increments of time. Eddies of sensible distractions for him were getting increasingly hard to find.

So I responded with the first thing that shot out of my mouth, "Bullshit, George! We cleared it."

"I can't help it, Angel. I'm not doing anything. They're just so . . . fresh. Their skin is so fresh."

Trembling, I braced myself against the kitchen counter as a fearful vision crept into my brain. I saw one of the boys catch George's eye and freeze. He was paralyzed with terror, unable to run. I heard his heartbeat pounding in my ears and felt his horror stinging his chest. As the top of my head began to sting, I heard my guides say, *"No Gina! Don't let him!"*

"Georrrrrrrge!" I shrieked. "The first time you get an erection in years, and you get it from looking at children playing? Do you hear what you're saying? Leave the park and go back to watching porno George! Now! I swear to you—I'll call the cops! Tell me you're leaving the park!!"

"Angel, calm down. Calm down. I'm leaving, Angel. It was just a moment. Just a thought. I'm leaving. I'm leaving. There, there, sweet Angel. Were you worried? Did I scare you? I'm sorry I scared you."

But I was still hysterical. "You're scaring the shit out of me, George! I want to hear your car start. I want to hear it, George! Start your car, and leave that place right now! We'll stay on the phone. Just please get the hell out of there and get in your car and go home!!"

I remember thinking, *What did I do wrong? What happened? Was the mal occhio trying to mess with me? Should I call the police?* I needed help. George was unlike any of my clients. For the first time since I got my gift, I felt insecure about my ability. Honestly, this was far more than I'd ever handled. George's problems were rooted in years and years of abuse and *mal occhio.* Dealing with a desire to have sex with children had *never* been a part of my psychic world.

My clients feel that they can call me whenever, wherever and I will respond to their pain. I feel obligated to listen when clients say they're going to kill themselves or hurt somebody else. And when the therapist or psychiatrist is already at home, having dinner with her kids, I am still taking phone calls from freaks like George.

Therefore, I made it a point to answer every phone call from George just to make sure he wasn't hurting anyone. But I made a mistake. I called him and said, "George, are you still thinking about the little boys?"

"I was always attracted to younger guys, but not this young. I have faith in you. You're going to help me," he said. "I know I'm a piece of work. You really got your hands full. When this is over I'm going to give you a wonderful present."

I said, "The best present would be for you to call me and tell me you have normal urges for adults. That you really are better and you're happy."

He said it was time for him to prepare dinner and call his mother, so I hung up. I felt them talk about me . . . I could hear it . . . in my head.

"Who is this girl . . . this tramp you talk to, George?" his mother said.

"Don't talk about Angel like that!"

"Oh! Angel? That's the hooker's name?"

While I was "hearing" this, I started worrying. *Oh shit! I told this sick bastard personal stuff about my life.* In the course of treating George, I had given birth to a boy, and we had talked about the baby.

I wasn't seeing any improvement in George. He gave me every sick little detail about his sordid desires, daily. After a life of abuse and the family *mal occhio*, I understood he would have to let a few demons out— but this was ridiculous.

It struck me, and I know this sounds absurd, that he was experimenting with any and all sick sexual thoughts he could force himself to dream up. George was actually inviting demons in.

I lay on my bed that night praying for hours. One day, I thought, *I have to get rid of this pervert.* I began to work on his father, to get his dad to show him a little goodness, and take the stress off George so he wouldn't need to escape. I purified his father by covering him with prayer and included George in the process. I rebuked all the evil spirits from him, and I asked God to intervene and cover his soul. I did a binding on the father. I bound him from doing or saying anything harmful to anybody else—almost like a kindness spell. The father, who I saw as the catalyst of George's sickness, changed within two weeks.

"Angel you did it again!!" George said.

We talked about the age-old secret, "When two or more souls are gathered, praying in God's name, He listens. The prayers of a righteous person are always heard."

But George's mother, who also noticed the change, lashed out at me.

"Why are you always talking to that hooker?" she'd ask him. "Are you gonna defy us and keep living like the weirdos in Miami? People in Miami are nothing but whores! What are you paying her, George? She doesn't care about you! She's a whore! What does she know about us? She's going to come out here to our house and rob us, thanks to you, George!"

Finally, completely at his wit's end, George told his mother that he was paying for my services as a psychic. His mother stopped speaking to him.

"Angel, Mom won't call me or answer any of my calls! I can't deal with this. Is this normal? Would you speak to her, Angel?"

"Yes, George. I want her to know nothing else is going on. I'm just doing my job as a psychic. It wouldn't hurt her to hear how this life has hurt you."

We called his mother from my phone on a three-way party line. She answered the phone and hissed "hello." She said she was very curious. I said I understood, that it was a mother's job to know what's happening in her child's life. I told her who I was and that I was a master psychic and I was trying to help her son.

"Help him with what?" she said.

"He's a grown man who does not go out, has no significant other and no children. Oh yes—and his erections are brought on by depravity—by porn and kids. Does this sound normal to you?" I asked.

"I don't understand what you mean," she said.

"Is it that you truly don't understand or that you just don't want to understand?"

Then she got testy. "I don't like your tone of voice," she said.

"In the world I live in, a grown man whose parents have been very abusive to him and who now watches little boys to get an erection has a problem. Do you even know how sick George is?" I asked.

"Sick? What sick? What's wrong with George? How much are you charging him?"

"That's private and confidential."

His mother hung up, and George freaked out.

I said, "George, you know your mother has a codependency problem.

Your mother tries to plant things in your head—like having a need to talk to her every damn day. Do you realize how much damage this has done to you? You need to get out. And I need a break. George, I'm going to go on a spiritual fast. I need to be one with my spirits and my guides before I go any further."

So I stopped talking to him for one week. About ninety FedEx packages piled up in my office next to my computer. I never got to open them because I was praying and fasting. He also called about every fifteen minutes, but I didn't answer. I don't allow myself to be distracted. George's spirit guides would not come to me, and I could not reach them. Something would not allow me to get in. One morning I finally opened the "dream" letters inside the FedEx packages.

Inside my head, I heard a deafening crash. Like a glass chandelier, falling and shattering. I called him and said, "George, you are in a place too dark for me to enter."

"No, don't say that!! Look how much my life has changed, for God's sake! Angel please!!! Don't abandon me!!!"

"George, it's over. You've completely given up your life to darkness, and I can't follow you in there, no matter what you say to me, no matter what you pay me. You are an instrument of evil. You've fooled me long enough, George! These depraved things are giving you the energy to live and breathe. But you're dead, George."

I hung up the phone. I swear on my life I have never seen such ghastly rage, such madness, and such unlamented evil in all my life. This man was caught by the unmerciful master. He was now dead inside—dead to the core. In the letters were detailed accounts of his desires to have sex with me and my infant son. He wrote about kidnapping boys, tying them up in a hotel room, and doing unspeakable things to them. He wrote about seeing a therapist, but she'd made him feel it was all in his mind. He wanted it to be in his life. He didn't want normal desires. He had no desire to be normal.

I did the only thing a confused Gypsy psychic could do. I consulted our *Baro*. There are one million Gypsies in America, about whom most people know nothing. Ten thousand of them live in South Florida. Gypsies have been coming to the United States for centuries. They rowed the ships for early European explorers. They escaped slavery in nineteenth-century Romania. They fled Nazi gas chamber Roma genocide. They were the only other ethnic group, along with the Jews, to be exclusively singled out for extermination.

So we hide. We are *under* the law. We consult our own leaders for "legal" help. The *Baro* is the male Gypsy community leader. He understands the origins of our traditions and how and why ancient Rom law has defined our way of life. He negotiates between community barriers and our fears of persecution, deciding, for instance, when to risk calling the cops. Some police officers declare themselves experts on "Gypsy crime." It's futile to try to defend yourself against them. He was the only person to trust in the matter. The *Baro* takes it to the crypt. After listening to my bizarre story for hours, "sick bastard" were his only words. The *Baro* took the information and spread the word among the Gypsies not to deal with this sick bastard, but sadly, did not tell the police.

Soon, George's lawyer contacted me demanding I return all the letters and give back all the money George paid me. Of course, that's what some clients do when they get busted. All of a sudden I'm the freak, a scam artist who stole George's money and made him write the letters. He told the lawyer that I dictated each word and forced him to sign each letter.

Somehow, I found Willie Tiger, a lawyer who would take me on. He was a fourth-generation Seminole from the Big Cypress Swamp reservation. Tough and clever, he understood bigotry and racial profiling. My lawyer arranged a private meeting with George's lawyer and threatened to go to the media, and all of Miami, with the letters. George caved and backed off. I burned the letters, cleansed the ashes, and buried them in a compost pile out on Virginia Key. I didn't want anything from George in our house. I kept the Bentley I bought with some of the money George paid me, but returned the rest.

George's dreams never came true. He solicited sex from an undercover cop over the Internet and landed in jail.

SEVEN

Bagel Break

New Yorkers always say they can never find a good bagel in Miami. I'm a New Yorker, and I don't agree. All of the New York Gypsies loved Bagel-Rama. They made one helluva good bagel. Luckily, they were located on just about every corner, so you could get one fast and fresh.

My favorite location was one in an Aventura strip mall, right next to my nail salon. Every Tuesday, before I got my nails done, I stopped in. The nail salon was very popular, and the Bagel-Rama owner's wife, Gianna, a beautiful brunette, with a slim build and a mane of thick, wavy chestnut hair, frequented it. One day we sat next to each other in the massage chairs, getting pedicures; each of us conversing with our pedicurist. And I heard the magic words: "I feel like someone's out to get me."

"What makes you think that?" I piped in, completely ignoring pedicure protocol.

"Excuse me?" she asked.

"I'm sorry to interrupt, but weren't you saying that you thought someone was out to get you?"

"I'm sorry? . . . Yes, but I uh . . ." she said, timidly.

"I can help you with that," I said. "I can remove all curses, *mal occhio*, bad luck, anything."

My pedicurist, Sylvia, from the Dominican Republic looked up. "She can. She's the best. She's a psychic. She helped me with my daughter. *Madre de Dios!* She had so many problems with men. Then she found a good boyfriend. He was a good man. The first good man she had ever been with. All the rest were *cabrones*. But she didn't want to marry him. Regina did some work for me. And now she's married, and I have two grandchildren," Sylvia said proudly.

Staring earnestly at me with her deep brown eyes, Gianna said, "Do you think you could find out what's been giving me terrible nightmares? If you could help me, I would give you everything I have. I never have any peace. *Never.* Could you help me?"

I knew then she wasn't exaggerating. I got the feeling this would be a lot of work.

"Yes, I can. Come to my office, right around the corner. Come in right after you finish here!" I encouraged her.

Later that afternoon, in my little office, I heard the bells tinkling at the door. Gianna let herself in and timidly asked if anyone was there. I emerged from my makeshift prayer room and sensed my guides telling me she was right about her fears. So I told her something no one else could know—information only my spirit guides could provide.

"I have a feeling you're on a lot of drugs. Prescription medication," I said.

She explained that her doctors had given up on her. Unable to determine what was causing her strange dreams, they medicated her to the eyeballs. She had been on every antidepressant you could imagine, but she wasn't depressed. She was on antianxiety pills at this point in time, but she wasn't paranoid. She was also drinking heavily.

Gianna's story began about twenty years ago, when she first arrived in New York from her native Italy. She'd met her husband, Gerry, in the restaurant where she worked as a waitress. He came from a very wealthy Jewish family, who already owned several delis and bagel bars across Manhattan. Her family came from a small town and didn't have a penny. But Gianna was intensely beautiful, the type of all-natural beauty that makes men want to breed. She had olive-tan skin and pouty, rose-colored lips. He showered her with gifts and extravagant outings. Eventually he swept her off her feet. She got pregnant; they married and moved to Miami.

Life moved blissfully along until a few years ago, when Gianna brought her aging father to live in Miami. He was very old, but not ill, when he arrived. She set him up in a little Spanish-style house in Coral Gables and got him a live-in maid, Anatola, from Colombia.

Then things started to go wrong. Gianna felt everything in her life that meant something to her was slowly being destroyed. Her father became very ill, and doctors could not identify the problem. Her son and daughter, both of whom were married, had babies who were born prematurely at eight months. Both babies died after three days. Her husband began an affair with a girl who made bagels at one of his stores. So many bad things happened to her in such a short amount of time, she believed she'd been the victim of *brujeria*, or black magic.

"But every time I tell Gerry that I don't like Anatola," she said, "that I feel she's doing something bad to me, he just jokes that maybe I want her sexually, but she doesn't want me. His family keeps telling him I've snapped because the kids are gone, because I lost my grandbabies. They're too powerful for me to fight them on this thing, and they've labeled me a lunatic."

In order to suppress her gut feelings and to quash the anger she felt about her husband's ridicule, she started hitting the vodka pretty regularly. Her maid Roxana, who hailed from Havana and who'd been with Gianna for nearly twenty years, agreed it was *brujeria*.

Roxana raised both of Gianna's kids, took care of Gianna during her drinking binges, and was a trusted confidante. She told Gianna to see Walter Mercado, an internationally known psychic based in Miami, but he scared her. She said he was too weird. He dressed like a sorcerer. She felt he was a demon.

Then Gianna burst into tears and described to me in great detail how she saw her dead grandbabies weeping while she slept. She felt they had been injured in some way. She said every time she spoke to her father on the phone she felt nauseous. Something about the maid Anatola at her dad's house freaked her out.

"I can't focus!" Gianna said, hysterically. "She's doing bad things to us. My sister has just been diagnosed with breast cancer. My brother just had a heart attack, and he's in the hospital in New York. I'm killing myself with alcohol! She's doing this so there'll be no one to say she killed Dad! She's killing us all, Regina! Can you help me?"

I asked if she'd seen any rotting fruit inside the house, under beds, under sinks, anywhere. Gianna said she had.

"I think I saw something like that under my father's bed. And there was some kind of dish with imported candies behind the kitchen door," she said.

"I think the woman in your dad's house is not a real nurse. It does sound like she's practicing Santeria. She is trying to hurt your father. I know this sounds pretty bad and crazy, too, but you need to go to his house. I saw lots of legal papers when I threw the cards down. She wants him to sign some papers. Now she's made him sick. She is really, really evil, Gianna. We need to do a protection shield on you, but you have to get the papers."

I started to help her on a weekly basis. I began by praying with her to help her release the anger she had for her husband. Then I set aside hours of Reiki a day to encourage spiritual healing and some energy balancing, for her insomnia. This we did at my house.

Gianna had a breakdown a few weeks into Reiki. It was 1:00 A.M., and Romy and I were sleeping. The phone rang off the hook. It was Roxana. Gianna had drunk a bottle of vodka and taken a bunch of pills. She was passed out. The maid couldn't find Gerry. I called 911 myself. Gerry had disappeared, and Gianna had tried to commit suicide. As I drove to the Aventura hospital to meet the paramedics, it occurred to me that, based on what Gianna told me, committing suicide would have left her father completely helpless and alone. Because Gianna was the only one who sus-pected foul play. This wasn't consistent with her agenda. When I got to the hospital, she was alert and well, so I asked her what happened.

"Regina, all I remember is that Gerry told me I was a spoiled drunk bitch and to get a life because I did something that's totally unlike me!"

"What did you do?"

"Something told me to give away all my clothes to the poor. I took all my Fendi, Louis Vuitton, Chanel, all my beautiful clothes and shoes and pocketbooks, and gave it to Goodwill yesterday. The one over in Hialeah. And now I'm like, 'What the hell did I do that for?'"

"Were you drinking, Gianna?"

"No—No!! I swear, Regina! I had a lunch date with some friends and then a hair appointment. You know I don't drink when I have to be around other people! I was stone sober. I was in some kind of a trance."

"Where was the Goodwill?"

"In Hialeah, over on Lake Patricia Drive."

"There's a *voodoienne* that has a shop on Lake Patricia. Her name's Erzulie."

"What do you mean? Is Anatola calling on voodoo to destroy me? Oh my God! What do you mean, Regina? God help me! She's going to kill me. I knew it! And nobody believes me!"

"Gianna, calm down. It's going to be okay. Go to your dad's house to-day. Don't call—barge right in. Look in the kitchen, in the bathrooms, under his bed, in the desk drawers, everywhere. When you find any traces of any legal documents, call me immediately. Do you understand? You must call me the minute you find any of those things!"

She called me that night crying hysterically. She found some insur-ance policy with her dad's signature. She guessed some sort of scam was afoot. We visited Erzulie the next day. That morning, the air was packed with large, buzzing, shimmery turquoise dragonflies from the Everglades. They were hitting the windshield of her Jaguar as we drove west over to Hialeah. All the way there she cried and cried. She was so scared. I knew a little about Erzulie. Everyone in Miami's heard about her. She's expensive, but she's fair. I kept trying to reassure Gianna that Erzulie wasn't after her. She was after the money.

"Gianna, listen to me, I swear, everything I've ever heard about Erzulie is that she's a very good businesswoman. She's never in it for anything but the money, and she does whatever she's asked to do. She's really good at what she does, but she can be bought and she knows it. If she'd wanted to kill you, you'd already be dead. She already knows you have more than Anatola will ever get. She knows the outcome, and she's wants to flush you out."

"I don't know why I have to go, too. Can't you just go in and take care of this yourself? I'll give you any amount you need. I'll give you a blank check. Just let me stay in the car."

"Calm down, Gianna. Listen to me, first of all, don't even mention checks. She doesn't take them. Erzulie is a woman who honors her business contracts. She needs to see you have respect. She'll want to look you in the eye. She won't know how much she wants to charge, until she sees *you*. That's the way it works. You have to maintain your composure. If she sees you're hysterical, she won't help because you'll show your weakness. Okay, look there's the little botanica. Turn left here and park. Don't panic, no matter what she says at first. Let me do the talking, but be ready to hand over some serious cash. Did you bring cash?"

"Yes."

"Okay, then, let's go in."

We walked in the cramped ghetto store through a side doorway. It was cluttered and dark and smelled of patchouli and rum. Drumming and chanting came from a small tape player on the windowsill, calling the voodoo deities, the *loas*.

A glass counter case filled with tarot decks, amulets, and potions was on our end of the entrance, followed by rows of special candles, oils, beads, books in Kreyol (Creole) and statues. At the end of the narrow store was a pit, cordoned off by a sash. A copper dish was filled with imported candies and pennies. Three small piles of incense burned around the dish, and an open bottle of rum stood against a huge statue of the *loa* Maitre Carrefour, the "patron saint" of sorcerers and of the cross-roads. I knew because I smelled him. It was the rum. Erzulie was wrapped in a dingy yellow sarong with a matching headwrap. She sat hunched on a stool at the end of the dark pit, fanning herself with the torn-off top of a cardboard box. She was very black, with black eyes, roly-poly, and bare-foot. There she was, in all her fleshy glory, fanning away, grinning and waiting.

"'Ow can I 'elp you, mes dames?"

"Hello. My name is Regina Milbourne, and this is my client, Gianna Eisenberg. We're looking for Madame Erzulie. We'd like to talk business with Madame Erzulie."

"She is not 'ere. Is deh something I can do foh you?"

"No thank you. Our business is only with Madame Erzulie. Do you know when she'll return?"

"No."

"Okay, well, thanks. Please tell her we came by, Gianna Eisenberg and Regina Milbourne. We can be reached at this number . . . do you have a pen I can borrow?"

"No. But my bwotha, he 'ave won."

At that moment I noticed the thin black boy, in the shadows next to the merchandise. Wearing only navy blue shorts, he had round, high buttocks and pronounced calves. He was skinny all the way around, with a really round head. He came forward, shy and watchful. He produced a pencil with the eraser chewed off. I took a sheet from the counter, wrote my cell number on the back of it, and handed it to her.

"Well, thanks again. Please have Madame Erzulie call us as soon a she can."

As soon as we were back in the Jag, she called.

"'Ave your fwend stay in the car and come in to speak to me."

Gianna was freaked out. She didn't want to sit alone in that neighborhood all by herself, but I had to leave her. When I got inside, Erzulie handed back the sheet of paper with her price on it. I was relieved every-thing went so smoothly, but I knew Gianna would have a fit when she saw how much this was going to cost her. Erzulie was going for her retire-ment. Without much hope, I went back to the car.

"They're dressed in rags! How much could she possibly want?" Gianna said.

"Five hundred . . . *thousand* . . ."

"What?! How the hell am I supposed to get that kind of money? What is she trying to do to me? I don't have that kind of money! I'd have to ask Gerry, and he'll throw me in an asylum! That bitch! Isn't there any-thing you can do instead? I've been paying you thousands for more than six months. You two are in on this together! What a bunch of shit! I'm not paying one dime!!"

"Look, Gianna, you can't put a price on your life. My light work isn't penetrating. She's really powerful, but yet, she's still willing to compro-mise. Think about what you've been going through and how long it's been since you felt really well."

"Forget it, Regina. This is all bullshit. My husband was right! I'm crazy. We're out of here!"

She peeled out of the parking lot without even letting me tell Erzulie she thought the price was too high. She was impatient, irritated, and hos-tile. My reputation was at stake. Erzulie and I worked the same area. I was very disappointed in Gianna—in both of them, to be honest. Both ex-hibited greed and ingratitude and a compete lack of control. I swear to God, people wear me out.

At 4:00 A.M., Gianna called. As I reached for the phone, I got a vision of an old man with bruises all over his face. Gianna was crying hysteri-cally. She said Anatola had called her and said her father had died in bed. I told her this was not true. Anatola beat him up and pushed him out of the wheelchair. She was probably sick of waiting. I told her to get an au-topsy immediately. I told her I saw bruises on his face in my visions.

It was late the next day when she called and said she had gone to see the body. Sure enough, there were the bruises, right on his forehead and chin. Anatola then said he'd slipped getting into the bathtub and died. The funeral was scheduled soon after, and she hadn't accomplished anything. Her dad was dead, and she was drinking heavily.

She tried to prevent Anatola from coming to the funeral. When that misfired, she lunged at Anatola during the funeral, making herself look stupid and violent to everyone. That week was lost. She fell into more drinking. I didn't hear from her except for two incidents when she called drunk from her cell phone. Finally after three weeks, she called and said she wanted to go see Erzulie.

"Gerry thinks I'm worse than ever, Regina, because I put a private detective on Anatola! But guess what he found out? The bitch is having lesbian parties over there at Dad's house! Gerry's allowing her to remain there until she can find another position! I got in a fight with him and asked him why he is letting that lesbian stay in the house, *when he knows she killed my father*! He says I'm crazy! I'm not even allowed to search for anything! Why is he doing this to me?? Is he trying to kill me, too??!! He lied to me and told me she was going to be outta there!! Today I got a call from a rehab in North Florida. Gerry's trying to put me away so he can go fuck his teenage mistress full-time. I can't take it anymore, Regina! I want to die! I just want to die! Please help me! Should I go back to the voodoo lady? I think I need to beg her to lower the price! I know I can get two hundred and fifty thousand. Would she take it?"

"Let me try to talk to her, Gianna. I think she's asking too much, also, and she did not kill your dad—Anatola did. Anatola got impatient, and now Erzulie is probably pissed off. Let's just go and talk to her, see what she says. She's not unreasonable."

So we showed up on Lake Patricia Drive again, but this time the store was closed. The boy was sitting on the threshold outside. He stood as soon as we drove up. He walked to our car and motioned us to follow him. We pulled back out of the parking lot driving really slowly because he wouldn't get in our car. For two blocks we tailed him, and then he turned into a pink stucco house with four mutts howling in the front yard. Erzulie came out the door with her hand on her hip, waiting for us. Gianna got out first and waved the fistful of cash at Erzulie. I thought, *Oh boy, here we go.* Erzulie was looking at me, and I waved and smiled. She waved us into her damp, smoky house, and we sat on a plastic covered sofa.

"Sit doaun mes dames," Erzulie said.

"I don't have five hundred thousand dollars, Miss Erzulie. I only have two hundred and fifty thousand. You already killed my father. I don't care anymore about myself. This is just so you'll stop fucking with my kids or their kids. I don't have the stomach for this anymore. You bitches can go rob someone else! I don't give a shit—I'm not paying another cent to either you or Regina. I just want it to end. I just want it to end."

"I did not keel anywan. Yoo caretaker killed yoo fatha, she beat him up, awound 'is 'ead. Yoo know dat alwedy. Yoo know why yoo 'ere. Yoo can bargahn wid me all yoo want, but you cannot 'elp yooself without Erzulie 'elp."

"Ladies, let's be rational about this. Erzulie, my client has had a terrible wrong done to her and her father. I know you are not a malicious person, Erzulie. You are a savvy businesswoman. I understand your position, but I must beg you to consider my client's loss. She is under heavy medication. She's not herself, and she is in no condition to truly appreciate what you are offering her, Erzulie. You know that under your protective shield and mine, she will soon see things clearer and give credit where it's due."

Eventually, Erzulie gave in, and Gianna gave her the two hundred and fifty thousand. Erzulie gave me 20 percent, the usual cut on referrals between spiritualists. She undid all the spells and spiritual restraints on Gianna's family.

Within six days, Gianna got off the meds and the booze. Her family's health improved. Her children were, again, expecting babies. A few weeks after visiting Erzulie, the coroner indeed found the her father's bruises were not compatible with Anatola's story. Before Gianna could get a warrant for her arrest, Anatola skipped town—probably back to Colombia. Gianna's peace of mind was restored, and that, to her, was unmistakably, magic.

EIGHT

The Husband, the Wife, and the Mistress

From time to time, I'd get repeat clients whose sexcapades were so, well, predictable, I used to joke with myself that one day they would overlap. They were mostly men: men who had trouble getting sex from their wives. Men who felt emotionally cut off by their wives. Or men who simply longed to bring the fun back into their relationships. Back before they had kids. Before their wives became puritanical, tyrannical, and *drab*. They'd get frustrated, and they'd fall in love with someone else. Then the love triangles would begin because the guys *wouldn't* leave their wives and *couldn't* stop seeing their girlfriends. Occasionally, one would be a *real man* and get a divorce. For the most part, the weak ones would stay married and keep returning to the same mistress because guys will come back *consistently* if they get what they need. And what they need is sex, of course: the best kind of sex—with someone they know and who knows them and their faults and fears and wants to please them, even in latex underwear. I have found that for men, it's all about letting their guard down, *at last*. It has nothing to do with being sexy, beautiful, thin, or rich. Good sex has everything to do with the comfort zone.

Sherry wasn't hideous, but she wasn't pretty. She was average-looking: average height, average hair. She came from an average-income family. Not wealthy, but not poor. She wasn't smart or dumb. Nothing special. She was really nice, though, and sometimes funny. I think what struck me most about Sherry is that she was just comfortable to be around—*soft* and not intimidating.

Sherry had a gorgeous boyfriend while she was in college here in Miami. She was studying to be a teacher. Her boyfriend, Jordan, was studying to be an architect. He was tall, athletic, with green eyes and thick, black, curly hair. People said he looked like JFK Jr. He and Sherry dated all through college. They were both Jewish, and Sherry expected they would get married. She really, *really* loved him. She wanted to have babies with him right after college. But architects and teachers don't make much money, and Jordan had other plans. He met a wealthy Jewish-American princess at a frat party toward the very end of his last year at college. She was attractive, intelligent, and spoiled. She "stole" his heart. He left Sherry in the dust. He and the new girl had a huge wedding and invited all their mutual friends. Soon after, he started a new life with his new wife, Tara. It crushed Sherry. She was asked out by some of their mutual friends, but she felt she couldn't trust anyone. She was depressed. She simply wasn't attracted to anyone else. She became a teacher and lived in an apartment in Coral Gables—not fancy, but not tacky.

Jordan became an architect in a big firm, and he and Tara lived luxuriously on her family's money. They had a four-thousand-square-foot house in Coconut Grove, Volvos and Beemers, a beautiful sailboat docked at Grove Key Marina, and two gorgeous kids who looked exactly like him. The Miami dream.

The story should end here, with me doing a cleansing for Sherry so she could move on to live a better life. But it doesn't. Sherry, Jordan, and Tara suffered from a condition worse than blindness: seeing something that isn't there.

Jordan came back to Sherry right after the honeymoon. They started having sex again. The first year, he told her he couldn't leave his wife because she was pregnant. The second year, he said he was focusing on his career, so he couldn't leave her then, either. The third year, his wife was pregnant again, and he had to stay. The fourth year of his marriage, *and of his affair with Sherry*, he was getting a promotion that involved a lot of travel, and he couldn't handle a divorce at the same time. And so on and so forth—there was always an excuse. He couldn't take Sherry out. He couldn't take Sherry on his trips. He came over three times a week—Mondays, Wednesdays, and Fridays—to have good, old-fashioned monkey sex and *snuggle*. Sherry lived in the Gables, right next to the Grove. It was all so convenient. He really could be in two places at once. He'd come straight from work, screw Sherry, and be home in time for a late dinner. Jordan was dashing and had a magnetic personality, appearing and disappearing, and leaving upheaval in his wake.

After thirteen years of this, Sherry resigned herself and adopted other plans. Because "pleasures, seldom reached, are once again pursued," Sherry came to me and said that she wanted me to help her have a baby. She told me Jordan had promised her that if he didn't leave his wife after ten years, he would give her his sperm. He promised he would be her sperm donor only and never have another baby with his wife. He also promised he would help her take care of the baby. He would be the partner she needed to raise that baby.

She said, "I don't want a reading. I don't want anybody else. I don't want another man. I just want a baby. I'm going to fight to get pregnant. Can you help me get Jordan to stop wearing a condom when we have sex?"

"Sherry, I think your problems stem from the fact you have no clue what or who you are," I began. "You are a mistress. As such, you are entitled to certain things. As a mistress you must love, honor, and cherish only one man for the rest of your life. You may never cheat on him. You may never confront his wife or children. You may never spend Hanukkah, Christmas, or other significant holidays with him. You will never celebrate his birthday on that day. You can never visit him in the hospital if he's sick, and you won't be there at his last breath. These things belong only to his wife and family. Mistresses are the true love of a man's life. You have the right to bear him children. You are entitled to financial assistance, such as your rent or mortgage, a car, any trips you want to take, expensive jewelry, art or cultural classes, hobby supplies, and anything you can think of that would make your life easier while waiting for him. He should also be able to bequeath property to you and your children. If he cannot afford any one of these things, he cannot afford a mistress and must either divorce his wife or stop seeing you. You have not been exercising any of these rights, and that's why he treats you like shit. Wife or mistress, either/or—but the man must take responsibility. Otherwise, you're not even fit to wear a whore's shoes."

Her jaw dropped.

"Now, I can help you have a baby, but seeing how you *never* laid down the law with this idiot, are you prepared to keep this baby and be able to take care of it even if Jordan doesn't keep his end of the bargain? Because I hate to break your heart again, but up to now, he hasn't exactly kept a promise to anyone but himself. I am not in the business of making babies so they can be aborted, put up for adoption, or otherwise abused," I said, straight up.

She said, "I've saved a little money. I'm earning good money in the school system. I have great benefits, and my mom said she'll help me, too. I really want this baby, Regina. If I can't have Jordan, then I want a little part of him I could love, that would truly love me back."

"That's not guaranteed."

"I know. I mean, someone I could love on a full-time basis. Someone I would be able to hold, when I want to, not three times a week, in the afternoon."

"What do you want for this child?"

"I want to love it. That's all. To love it and give it all the love I have inside of me that I can't give to anyone else," she said, with huge tears rolling down her face. She was sincere. She did have a lot of love inside her for this baby. So I went into meditation. My guides revealed that a baby did indeed want to come and that it wanted her as the mother. I saw this as a consolation prize for her, after being so loving and loyal to Jordan for so long. The scenes of maternal love I saw for her in meditation were all I needed. I decided to help her.

"I can do a ritual for you. It will be a love spell that will make him relax and sleep with you without a condom. It's very expensive. Can you afford twelve thousand dollars?"

"Yes I can! I've been saving up for something special, and this beats the crap out of a European vacation!"

"Okay, then, we begin like this," and I closed my eyes, held out my hands, palms up, and recited, "If you love someone who is married or has a child with a person other than you, then this ritual must be performed in order for another covenant to occur. I need a handwritten letter, in black ink on parchment, describing in specific details the nature of the problem and what you wish to do about it. When you write it, you must be completely sincere and fully understand what you're asking: *You want a baby from a married man.*

"Then I will need thirty-five hairs off your head—plucked, not cut. I need all the first names and dates of birth in the love triangle: wife's, husband's, and mistress's. Seven tears on a paper napkin. Do not wash the sheets from Monday's tryst because I need his essence from them. I need something personal of his, like his bar of soap. I need a dozen red roses and one red candle for every year you've been alive. I need one red candle for every year Jordan's been alive.

"I will fast, light the candles, and pray intensely for three days before the night you decide you will try this spell, before you make love to him."

I took a deep breath and continued. "Your part is twofold: first, you can't see him on your regular schedule. This is meant to shake things up, so he's thrown off-kilter. Tell him you're busy, or sick, or anything on a Wednesday, so he can't see you until Thursday. He'll feel off, and that's when the spell will work best.

"Second, I'll give you a mixture of honey, sugar, and molasses in a big Tupperware bowl. You must soak in it for an hour before your 'date.' While you do your thing, I'll do mine. I'll work my magic to leave him dreamy and receptive."

While all these preparations went on, I got a call from an old client, saying she knew someone who needed a reading from me because she thought her husband was being unfaithful. I said I could see the referral on Monday morning.

The following week, the new client came to my office. She looked like a mouse. She had an overbite and wore glasses like Sally Jessy Raphaël's. She said her name was Tara. She said her husband, an architect, was always working late.

"I think my husband's having an affair. I know he's having an affair! I've known for a while now. Does he love me?"

I spread out the cards. "Nope." There wasn't a speck of love for her in that deck. There was comfort and luxury, fruitfulness, and motherhood—but no love.

"Well, I don't care," she said. "I love being a mom, I love my kids, and I'm happy. I want to be pregnant again. I want a baby girl. Will he stop doing what he's doing? Is there something you can do? Like a spell? Can you put a spell on him? I've heard love spells can work, and I never heard of them in New York, but in Miami, everybody does them!"

"But does that mean you should do it?"

"Why not me? I'm a good mom. I have plenty of money to take care of my kids. We live mostly on my money. I'm at home with them. Can you make my husband love me? Or is he in love with her?" she asked.

"Look, I can't lie to you. It would take a lifetime of spells and more money than you could ever have to make him love you. But we could get you pregnant for twelve thousand dollars."

"Hmmm . . . okay."

So I held out my hands, palms up, and recited the same words I had used for Sherry. The next week, I did readings at a show in Mayfair, a mall in Coconut Grove. It was a huge, catered holiday party for all the stores and offices. It only paid a small flat fee, but I was hoping I could attract a few new clients at such a lavish party.

The party was in full swing. There was an extravagant cocktail buffet with typical Miami/tropic food—mostly Caribbean and Colombian—*arepas de vieques, bacalao, arroz con pollo, pastelitos,* and starfruit tarts. Of course, there was salsa, merengue, and cumbia dancing. Together they created the irresistible energy of color and rhythm that is Miami. Everyone was getting plastered.

Assistants were flirting with their bosses.

I was sitting in the corner with my double latte, and no one had come up to me for a tarot reading. Free psychic readings from a master psychic, and *no one* was having one done! I was sitting there at my card table, reading my magazine, and the most handsome curly haired guy sat down and said, "Happy holidays, pretty lady! Are you the real deal?"

I looked up and said, "Why don't you find out?"

"Okay. Tell me my future."

Then, I recognized him from Sherry's photo. It was Jordan! I thought, "*Oh no*! I already know his story!" I didn't know what to do. So I spread the cards out on the table, and this is what I said: "My guides tell me you are surrounded by love and devotion but are taking it for granted. You are ignoring the real and longing for the indefinable. You suffer from apathy and disengagement from the world. There are two women in your life. They love you very much. You love only one, but you are married to the other. You love your children more than you could ever love any woman, and you are a good father. Your children provide you with personal fortitude and strength of character. They enable you to maintain order and control in the midst of chaos. You had many wives in a past life, and that's why you are comfortable living in two worlds. But I can't lie to you—the good karma that followed you into this world will soon come to an end. Through procrastination and indecision, you will sire disillusionment and the inability to bring a certain matter to a conclusion. These consequences will indeed rain down on your children."

He just sat there, his big, beautiful, green eyes welling up with tears. He said, "Thanks. I can see why you were hired to do this." He got up and walked away.

This run-in was not coincidence. I could see for myself that the Divine power had been keeping this man and wife together for a reason. Maybe the third baby had to be born—a child sent by God to do good work on earth. However, baby notwithstanding, the time had come for all this to change. Six months went by, and Sherry called and told me she was pregnant. But then, she said, that she had seen Jordan's wife at the grocery store in Coconut Grove and she was also pregnant.

"Regina, I swear I couldn't believe it, but you were right! He can't keep a promise to anyone but himself! She's having the baby around the same time I am. He's never going to care for my baby, but I don't care. And I'm done, Regina!! I'm totally done!! I have what I want, and I don't need him!"

"Well, he's still the father, and you must encourage a relationship between him and the baby for the baby's sake." I said.

"I know! I know! But what I mean is I don't love him anymore like that."

A few weeks later Sherry called me back and said that Jordan's wife found out she was the mistress and that Sherry was pregnant. He admitted the whole thing, and his wife kicked him out. Elated and relieved, Jordan then contacted Sherry and told her he could finally be with her. Sherry told him she didn't want to be with him, not by default, and that all the indecisiveness had finally killed the passion. Sherry no longer loved him. However, Sherry was going to file a paternity suit against him and would expect child support and help with the baby. Tara and Sherry had their babies in the same month. Both babies were perfect, healthy, gorgeous seven-pound girls.

Later that year, at the annual holiday party in the Mayfair Mall, Jordan made his drunken way to my table.

"Hey. Remember me? I came to you for a reading last year, and you gave me a doozy of a reading! I've been hoping they would invite you back this year. I normally don't believe in psychics, but you said something, that . . . well . . . really hit home."

"How can I help you?"

"I'm in love with this lady I dated in college. But, she's . . . she's mad at me, I think, because I wouldn't leave my wife for her when she wanted. But now that's over, and I wonder if you see her coming back to me?"

"Jordan," I said.

"How do you know my name?"

"Jordan, I've made a living from the skill of persuading others to take on responsibilities far beyond their capabilities. It's called *motivation*. As for you, you're a charming seducer, appearing innocent and sympathetic, but in fact, you are selfish, ignorant, and unfaithful. You had no idea how lucky you were to have a wife to maintain a home for your children and mistress to lust after. You were irresponsible to both. They took care of you, and you took it for granted. Your blessings were taken away because you looked true love in the face and told it to go away. *Bezake*! Sin! Or as they say in Miami, *pecado*! In any language, Jordan, you *will* face the backlash of this wickedness in your next life."

They say it's a sin to alter God's words in any way, shape, or form, but that day I made an enormous copy of the Ten Commandments with explanatory sentences immediately following, thereby addressing those words that might confuse some people, such as "thou shall not" or "adultery."

It went something like this:

1. Thou shall not have other gods before me = One True God.
2. Thou shall not take the Lord's name in vain = Don't call Me, unless it's an emergency.
3. Keep holy the Sabbath = A mandatory day off per week. It will decrease the stress that creates sin.
4. Honor thy father and mother = Stop blaming your mom and dad for the past and give thanks that you are alive.
5. Thou shall not kill = Walk away from anger. It'll keep you from getting cancer.
6. Thou shall not commit adultery = Do not have sex with a married person.
7. Thou shall not steal = Instead, try to provide a service or good deed for every blessing bestowed.
8. Thou shall not bear false witness = Do not lie. It will only confuse *you*.

9. Thou shall not covet thy neighbor's wife = Stop lusting after anyone other than your spouse.
10. Thou shall not covet they neighbor's goods = Want what you have.

I framed it and put it up in my office as a reminder to clients.

NINE

Guilt-Free ID

There are at least five thousand Gypsies in Miami. They all seem to know one another. They shop at Aventura Mall, eat at Joe's Stone Crab, and hang out at the Mandarin Hotel downtown on Brickell.

The Gyp princesses want to cook and clean for the rest of their lives. The men want to hold onto their fortunes. Once I started making money, I didn't want to be like the rest of the Gyps. I didn't want to be restricted to one school of thought. I didn't want any types of limits or boundaries on my personality. Gypsies raise their children with too many worn-out, useless dicta. I didn't want that for mine. It was not good enough. I wanted my own identity.

I wanted to be the highest paid and best psychic. While I waited for the big fish, I advertised in *The Miami Herald* and got an entirely professional set of clientele—surgeons, judges, and people from the entertainment industry.

One day I got a call from a record producer, Todd Green. There was a something in his voice that sounded paranoid, like he was hiding something or doing something really wrong. He would never talk straight out.

"Hi. My name's Todd. I wanted to see what you could tell me about myself."

I said, "If there's something you haven't let go of, let's take a look at it."

"I want to know if you can tell me a little about myself. Should I come to your office?"

"Yes, that's fine. Bring in a metal object you've had in your pocket for a while."

I did a session with him. I told him that I saw he was good person, but he was seriously struggling with karma because every time something good happened to him, something three times worse also happened.

For instance, he got a job with a major Latino record producing company that he'd wanted to work with for years. A week later the company was sued, and he was named in the suit. Consequently, the company totally fell apart, and he lost his job. On the day he was to clean out his desk, where he kept his expensive laptop, the building was demolished, and the laptop was destroyed. The rubble from the demolition spewed all over his new 7 series BMW and tore up the hood. When he went to buy dinner for his new boyfriend, the card didn't go through. When he called the credit card company to ask what was wrong with the card, the customer service rep said there wasn't anything wrong with the card. His date paid the check and never saw him again.

He wanted to find out why he had so much bad luck. I told him I needed to do a meditation. When he came back to the office a few days later, I told him there was something not right about his name.

"Is this your birth name? Todd Green?"

"No."

"What's your real name?"

"It's Jared."

I considered the name and saw it was a good name.

"Okay. I feel I like this name. When people hear it, it is meant for success, meant for security. But there's still a black cloud over your head."

"Exactly. Can you remove it?" he asked.

I have to tell you, while I meditated this is what came to me: I saw a little boy, or the vision of a little boy, around eleven or twelve in a blue T-shirt and blue shorts with a red stripe going down the side. The little boy's cheeks were bright red, and he was sweating profusely.

So I asked him, "Do you have a problem with a little boy who, maybe, died of a fever?"

He just put his head in his hands, "Oh my God! Oh my God! Oh my God!"

"You have to tell me what this is, or I can't help you." I said.

"It's a long story."

"You have to tell me," I repeated.

"It's my dead brother. Look I can't hold down a job or have any peace of mind. I have horrible nightmares! I wake up with a fever, sweating, and hearing voices, like hallucinations. The kind you get when you have a really high fever. I need to talk to you."

"Well, then it makes sense. Something happened. He's trying to get a message across to you!" I said.

"Can you tell me what it is?"

I said, "I need a picture of him or anything that belongs to him, something that came from him."

Jared left, and I drove home. Whizzing down I-95 in my Benzie, I saw the little boy again. Frightened and uncomfortable, he tossed and turned and fell unconscious. The next day, Jared brought the picture of his brother and mother, and I went into meditation to see what the spirits were telling me. It was revealed this little boy was not resting and not at peace with his brother. Jared needed to put him at peace.

I said to him, "I saw your brother again, and he passed out from the fever."

He burst into tears, crying and moaning hysterically. He was groaning and wringing his hands.

I asked him, "Did you have a hand in hurting him?"

He said, "I can't talk about it! I can't talk about it! I went to counseling for years. I've been to psychiatrists, and I've been on all kinds of antidepressants."

"Well, Jared, I can't help you unless we work together to reveal what is causing the bad karma. I truly want you to be happy. I think you can achieve happiness. But when you are guilty of something hideous and you feel that guilt, it seeps out of you. It seeps out of you and reveals itself. There's nowhere to hide when you've got bad karma. Now, you need to tell me, did you have a hand in hurting him? The little boy in the blue shorts with the red stripe?"

"Oh my God! That's what he was wearing when he died!"

I came to find out that he hated his younger brother, who was eleven at the time of the tragedy. He was always very jealous of him. The father abandoned them, and the mother was a day-care assistant who worked long hours. They had a sitter, an old woman who slept a lot, while she was supposed to be watching them. Jared said they were old enough that they could practically watch themselves. Until the day of the tragedy.

I said, "You need to confront this with my spirit guides."

Slowly he told his tragic tale of neglect and betrayal. This unfortunate and unnecessary incident happened on a day when the old woman caregiver went to buy groceries for his mother. He said his brother was very ill. The boy kept imploring Jared to call their mother. "Call Mom! You need to tell her I don't feel good!"

Jared told him, "You need to go back to bed."

One of Jared's favorite things to do was pick on his brother, which, though mean, wouldn't have hurt him if the boy hadn't been really sick. He hadn't been well for a couple of days, but now the fever really shot up. Jared didn't know enough to care. He left the little boy home alone and went out with a few of his friends. When the mother came home, the little boy was dead. Later they found out he had had meningitis!

"How long have you been seeing this image?" I asked.

"Three years," Jared said.

"Hmm. Well, it didn't look like a ghost," I said. "Jared, this boy was resting. What did you do to invoke this boy's spirit?"

"Nothing, I swear. This has haunted me since he died. I've been through a lot of counseling. My mother blamed me for my brother's death."

"The name Todd comes up when you talk. And the name Todd comes up when I look at the pictures! Jared, I feel like you're not being honest with me. Is this all there is?"

He finally broke down, and he said that for three years, he'd been using his brother's ID.

"Four years ago my boyfriend Lucio cheated on me, so I broke up with him. He was from Argentina, and he was so gorgeous. I loved him so much, Regina. I tried to win him back by buying him anything I could. He left me anyway, for some fucking cruise ship dancer. I had ruined my name and credit. My mother moved into an old folks' home three years ago. When I went into a closet, I found an old shoebox. It had my brother's photos and birth certificate and social security number. I took it as a sign. I thought my brother was giving me a sign he was here to help me. I swear, Regina, I thought he gave it to me, and I've been using my brother's ID. But . . ."

"But boy, were you ever wrong. Jared, this is not right, and I have reason to believe in your heart you're aware that what you're doing is wrong."

He broke down again.

"Okay! I'm getting unemployment in his name, and also, I, uh . . . I'm HIV positive, and I'm getting money from disability. They're gonna cut off my disability if you tell! Please don't tell anybody! I'm trusting you!" he said.

I said, "False pleasures, pursued in vain, twice, cost you your sanity. Look, Jared, I uncovered this, and I uncovered it for a reason. You have to break this bad karma and put your brother's soul to rest again."

It had become clear to me that his brother had never forgiven him for what happened that day. I knew I would have to do a séance with the brother's spirit to figure out how to put him to rest. We waited until dark, and I met him at the office. We lit white candles and asked my spirit guides to help us. We prayed, and I invoked his brother's spirit, tentatively, because I really don't like to do this. My guides revealed that Jared needed to do a ritual himself, in the water, to set the brother's soul free.

"*I* have to do this?" he said.

95

"*You* brought him back," I replied.

"So what do I do?"

"We're going to use a tender, but effective, old Cuban ritual from my friends the *Santeros*. First, you have to write a note—an apology, purely from the heart. You need to state how sorry you are and that you will do whatsoever you have to do to make it up to him. It has to have a picture of the both of you in it. And it has to say you love him, also purely from the heart. The note must be on a tray, with a special candle. You must also pray for his immortal soul, every night for the rest of your life. Put that also in the note, with the prayer, and set it free into the ocean."

That night, we went to Crandon Beach, with all his supplies. In Miami, this ritual and versions of it are so common, we ran into three others with their trays and candles. It was also All Souls' Day, a high holy day. It was a beautiful clear night, under a full moon with the stars brilliantly shining.

He said his prayers and stepped into the sea, still looking over his shoulder.

"Keep focused! Focus!" I shouted.

"I feel very uncomfortable doing this. I don't want to do this, Regina. I paid you five thousand dollars; why can't you do this? Please, Regina! Please!"

"Because I did not invoke his spirit! It was you who invoked his spirit, so it must be you who puts him *back* to rest. If you don't want to do this from the heart, then stop wasting my time! I'm only here because I thought this was destroying you."

He freaked out and almost lost the tray. I pulled him out and said, "Look, *do not* waste my time! I don't need your five grand. You need me!"

Psychically, I knew he was coming from the heart, but he had no guts. I was in no mood for a wimp. While the rest of the penitents were slipping into the water noiselessly, my client and I were arguing on the sand, while trying not to let the candle blow out.

"I just feel stupid, Regina!" he said, pushing the tray at me.

"Whatever, Jared. I'm going home!" I said, pushing him back by the shoulders.

"Okay! Okay! Don't go, Regina, I'm sorry; we just don't do this kind of thing in my world."

"Not your *world*—your *culture*. Your white culture doesn't do ritual. Why do white people always say '*world*?' It's not your '*world*!!'" I shouted.

"You're right."

He went in without so much as a whimper. As soon as Jared was waist deep, rain started pouring down on the penitents, signaling that they all had been redeemed. There's always a sign when you've been redeemed: a dove, a rainbow, or the sun shining on a rainy day. There will always be a sign. The next day, I gave him a thorough cleansing with white roses. I burned sulfur and sage, and I blessed him with the smoke all over his aura. I made him tell me from his heart and also in front of God, again, how sorry he was. Jared decided to move after our ritual. He decided Miami wasn't the place for him to begin all over again. He sold everything he could, packed up what was left, and flew to California.

While he was on the plane, he slept. He told me he dreamt he saw his brother in the water at the beach when they were both young. He said they were playing with each other, and his brother said, "Give me a hug, Jared." Although Jared was hesitant, he did it. Then, Todd started walking into the water. When he got up to his chest, he turned back and waved to him, smiling.

Jared promised me he would take care of the stolen identity thing. Later that year he called for another reading about love. He sent a check from "Jared Green" for three hundred dollars.

The check bounced, but at least it had his real name on it.

TEN

Georgia
Homeboy

In the nineties, "club drugs" hit Miami. Hot, young, fashion-conscious partygoers who took spinning classes at gyms and drank smoothies shunned traditional drugs like alcohol and cigarettes. They replaced them with Ecstasy and Georgia Homeboy (also known as GHB or the "date-rape drug"), costing twenty-five dollars a pop.

All the good stuff was coming from the Netherlands and being sold by the Russian Mafia, or as they liked to call themselves, the Red Mafia. They ran the rings on the beach, discreetly charging nonalcoholic juice-bar patrons hundreds of dollars at the entrance for a party-pack of narcotics to help them through their busy night of frenetic gyrating. Amazingly, the more the DEA busted the Reds, the more brazenly they smuggled the stuff aboard the airlines to all points south, often consulting with the South American cartels about which route was best into the gateway, Miami. Powerful and bloodthirsty, slicing through Miami culture with raw violence, these scum blended with the Israeli, Colombian, Cuban, Haitian, Jamaican, and Jewish Mafia with ease, selling anything to make a buck.

Sporting Caesar haircuts, tans, and guayabera shirts, they looked like the natives. The only telltale signs were their razor-sharp, pointy, yellow, crooked teeth. Psychics like me had to stay on our toes whenever the regular drug czars wanted protection spells because as soon as word got out that one spell worked, along came the Reds, with a hundred grand for a job involving three countries, two flights, and a superkiller-whacker (champion hit man). Some even requested spells for invisibility! Word on the streets for Santeros and such was to focus on love spells or take a vacation. Many *brujas* (panteres) fled to L.A.

Erzulie flat-out refused to conjure any orishas for the Reds. She used her quick tongue, which usually got her into trouble, to get herself out.

"Dey gwew up wis no God or spiwits," she'd say. "Godwess animals. Godwess. There is no sport in dat. Cannot summon *loa* spiwits wivout a belief in dem. No, No, No."

On the corner of the strip mall where I rented my little office space was a so-so day spa called the Shapely Sheba. At lunchtime, I'd go and get my acrylics filled for fifteen dollars by a Chechnyan girl named Lavinia. She had the thickest Russian accent I'd ever heard. Tall and blonde, she stood out at the spa like the random violet sticking out of a soft mossy blanket. And *she* would always compliment *me*.

"Oh Miss Regina, I love your purse! Is zat veal Chanel? I love your skirt! Vhat designer is zat?"

"Yes it's real," I'd say, giggling. I could see she truly did appreciate the labels.

One day, Lavinia asked me what I did for a living.

"I'm a master psychic."

"A vaht?"

"A psychic. A clairvoyant. A person who can predict things that will happen in the future."

"You vead the tarot?"

"Exactly."

"Oh Miss Regina, I need a veading. How much is it?"

"Lavinia, if you hook me up with a fill, I'll give you a reading. I've got the cards right in my purse," I said.

"Done." But she said she couldn't do it at the spa. "I don't vant you to vead me at the nail salon. I need you to vead me in private."

"Okay, come to my office after you're done."

A few minutes later she came into my office, and I spread out the cards. The cards showed me she was having an affair.

"Lavinia, I see you're flanked by two men. One is younger than you, he's your husband, and one is older, he's the man you're in love with."

"You're a vitch!"

"A what?"

"A vitch! A vitch! How do you know this? You are incredible!"

"Did you say 'bitch' or 'witch' Lavinia?"

"A vitch! With the black hat!" she said, making a pointing gesture to where the top of the hat would be.

"Oh. Okay. This guy you love, he's no good. There is a great deal of danger around this man. A lot of killing."

"Yah, I know that," she said.

"I see a lot of illegal things around this man. I see drugs."

"He gives me good shit. He drives me crazy in bed. And he alvays comes after me! Alvays."

"But you're with him just because he's got money."

"He's my husband's brother-in-law. I know he's not in love vith his vife. She is a vitch. The one vizout deh black hat! I hate my husband; I stay vith him just for my doter. I vant a divorce. I love Dima! Dima's the man I vant," she said defiantly.

"You're willing to get involved with a man like this? A superkiller-whacker? A drug-dealing pill pusher? And you have a little girl! Is he a Red?" I was shocked. Red Mafia are calculating, corrupt, no-bullshit scum.

"I vant you to vead Dima" was all she said.

"Lavinia, you have to stop."

"Waddya think? Is it not good for me?"

I just laughed and shook my head. "I'll see you next week for a fill."

"I vant you to vead Dima. Okay?"

"Yes. That'll be fine."

A week went by and no word from Lavinia. Then, on the day before my appointment, she called in hysterics.

"Vegina! Dima's vife busted in on us!"

Dima's wife found them making love at the Ritz in Key Biscayne. She and Dima were under the sheets while his wife crept in, quietly, and put a gun to Dima's head.

"Ve vent to the Vitz, to spend ze night. Dima made some calls and vent out for a few hours. Vhen he veturned, ve made love. Dima's vife busted in and put a gun to Dima's head. Dima vas naked, on top of me, and if she had shot it, it vould have killed me as vell! I was crying and screaming. She kept screaming, 'I'll kill us all vight now!' Dima shouted 'No! No! No!' and grabbed her hand, and ze gun vent off!! Before ze police came, ze two of us had to help Dima escape because . . . because he is . . . he is ze Georgia Homeboy supplier for Miami. You must never tell anyone you know who he is, or you vill also have to vorry someone vill kill you!

"Ze police came, and I had to lie and say ve vere the only vuns in ze room, and so did his wife! Luckily, she vas trying to choke me vhen zey came in! They calmed her down, took her to jail. Dima bailed her out already!"

I knew at that moment I was in trouble. Once I heard Dima was not only a Red, but also the Homeboy dealer, I was going to be asked for a protection spell—and God only knew what else.

The next day she came in with Dima in tow. He was fat and bald with a long, thin, greasy ponytail.

"Hello Regina. How are you doingk?"

"Fine thank you, Dima. Please sit down. What can I do for you?"

"Dima vants a protection spell," Lavinia blurted out. "He vent to psychic on Stirling Road, and she told him she needed five hundred thousand dollars for a protection spell. He vas just about to give it to her, but I don't know her. Dima has never had her vead for him. I know you are a veal vitch, Vegina. Ve vant you to do it."

"I have some people trying to kill me. My mother-in-law is trying to kill Lavi. My mother-in-law is one of the bosses. I am not drug dealer. She is drug dealer. She brings it into Miami. I am the superkiller," said Dima.

"So why would they want to hurt you?"

"Because of my vife. She is crazy. She's been nagging me to make more money and make more money. She never cooks. She is spoiled and rotten. I don't love her. She vants Lavi and me dead, and her mother is ze boss. She can always get another superkiller and son-in-law. Lavi knows too much. You don't understand zis people."

"Oh, but I do! In Gypsy culture, when a woman cheats on a man, the man gets everything—the house, the kids, the money. The woman's head is shaved, and she is dumped out on the street. We're bought by our husbands, Dima. I know full well what it's like to be chattel and, therefore, disposable. But I can't charge you any less than the first psychic. This is going to have to be a very powerful spell."

"My vife's mother is the head of Red Mafia in Miami. She hired me to get rid of any dealer who stood in her vay when the Red infiltrated the city. The only vuns who gave me any trouble vere the Haitian gangs, but no one ever notices when zey die, anyway. I killed a bunch of Haitians for her. I cut off ze arms, feet, and head, so no one identifies ze body. I throw ze trunks into ze bay and burn ze rest. She took over quickly and soon had no use for me. But I am married to her doter, and zat was my guarantee. I haven't vorked for a few years, and ve live off my vife. I take drugs to keep me from going crazy. I give some to Lavi, vhen I meet her at the salon, vhen I go to pick up my vife. Lavi and I fall in love."

"Uh-huh," I said, nonchalantly. I don't trust the Reds. None of them. They'd shoot you just to test their gun. For all I knew he probably already killed his wife, and she was stuffed in the trunk of his car. But I also didn't dare say no.

"How much?"

"A million."

"Vhoo!" he whistled. "Vow."

"That's right. I have lots to do. Many, many, many prayers and a trip to the cemetery."

"Fine. You vill have it."

"I'm also going to need two bullets from any gun and three drops of perspiration from your brow. Bring them to me next week."

That night, when I went into meditation on Dima, I heard a voice I assumed was his mother-in-law, vehemently calling Lavi a *prostutytka*. At 6:00 A.M. the next morning, Romy and I heard the doorbell ringing off the hook. Romy got up and went to check it out, thinking it was probably some kids. It was Saturday, and we lived in a very posh neighborhood on Hibiscus Island, where the kids were really spoiled and rotten. A few minutes later, Romy came rushing in.

"Gina, get up! It's the Russians."

I threw my robe and slippers on haphazardly and rushed downstairs. Dima, Lavi, and a little girl were in the doorway.

"Regina," Dima said, when they saw me on the landing, "You better guarantee us ve're safe! Ve need to be safe. Ve're fleeing to the islands today, and ve need a guarantee. If ve're not safe, zey'll come after you, too; you can bet on zat!"

"What's happening?"

"Dima's vife has gone to her mother. Everyone vill be looking for us. Get us out safely!"

"Last night, in my meditation, I heard your mother-in-law calling Lavi a *prostutytka*."

"My God! Yes! Zats what she calls me! A prostitute!" gasped Lavi.

It never ceases to amaze me when I blow their minds.

"Did you bring what I asked for?"

"Yes. Here's your fee. And ze bullets are from my own gun," said Dima, handing me a little brown paper lunchbag.

"Good. Good. Send word in one year to a man at the Miami Beach DMV called Sharkey. Just tell Sharkey, 'Red Light Go.' I want you to do that every year on the same day. If you encounter any trouble at all, say 'Green Light.' But you won't. Okay, be safe. God bless." I knew Sharkey would take this to the crypt. I ran back inside and threw on some jeans as they pulled away. I jumped in the Beemer and drove out to Cocoplum Cemetery.

Cocoplum Cemetery used to be the Pinewood Cemetery. It's a small, quiet grove of pine and mangroves at the end of Erwin Road, one hundred fifty feet south of Sunset Drive. Unmarked, it is where they buried the unidentified pioneer babies that died before the 1900s. It's a sacred, solidly defended place. Not many know about the spiritual benefits of such a place. There are nearly twenty innocent babies buried there, and their souls guard anything buried in Cocoplum Cemetery.

When I got there, I summoned the spirits to guard and protect them. Sand whirled up in little dust clouds at my feet. I heard the scuttle of mangrove rats and the herons start honking. I thought, *Good! It's working!*

I raised my hands and bowed my head over the bullets and the napkin with Dima's sweat. Releasing a tremendous power, I recited a sacred prayer calling for the highest level of safety and refuge.

I buried the bullets and napkin together, bound up by a hairnet, under the faded marker of the grave of the eldest baby. I prayed that no bullet would enter their bodies or brains.

Precisely one year later, and every year thereafter, the Reds sent word. Sharkey never tells me how or from where.

ELEVEN

Leggings and Keys

The Red's payment left me with a craving for Beluga caviar and an abundance of material prosperity and riches. Free from financial anxiety, I would have thought my life would be pure luxury and pleasure. But Romy and I were going through hell. Someone had put a curse on us. We started losing things. Important things: daily minders, wallets, even toothbrushes and car keys. No matter what tactic we devised to remind us where they were at night, they were never in the same place the next morning.

I meditated over and again on the subject, but to no avail. My guides weren't responding. Even they were lost.

Then one night I had a dream. In the dream, I was sleeping in our king-size bed, alone. Suddenly, the bedroom window slid open and in climbed the devil, wearing a Marlins cap and brown bomber jacket. He walked over to me and sat down at the foot of my bed.

"Gina, babe. G-money. Why won't you be mine? I've given you everything. Cars, jewels, houses, and this is the way you thank me? Tonight you'll repay me for all the bullshit!!"

He stood up menacingly and chased me all around and around the bed. Gasping, I dodged his grasp, if only by inches, and kept running. A foul odor awoke me, and I was soaked in sweat and exhausted, standing on the bedroom floor. I realized it was a warning.

Romy and I had recently begun to attend a nondenominational Christian church, where we had officially conferred our lives to God in a short ceremony. When Romy asked the pastor, who presided over the ceremony, what he thought about psychics, he had this to say:

"Micah the biblical prophet said God often threatens to smite those 'who plot evil in their beds . . . and covet,' but rarely does. In fact, when people turn penitent to God and offer Him 'burnt offerings, calves, ten thousands rivers of oil, or even a firstborn,' Micah said *they just don't get it*. 'He has told you what is good; and what the Lord requires of you is to do justice, and to love kindness.' You explore questions of passion and the inner workings of human reason. Whether you charge one dollar or one million dollars is irrelevant. The question is, are you helping people?"

The next morning, I was doing a reading at the Falls Mall, in a kiosk next to Bloomingdales, when I lost concentration because of the distant clinking and jingling of a key chain with hundreds of keys. Someone bulky, in a tremendous hurry, made a beeline toward me. She was wearing cherry-red spandex pants, Reebok sneakers, and an oversized T-shirt that said something about "bitch." I could hear her coming all the way from the entrance with *those keys*. Clink-clink ca-clink-clink ca-clink-clink.

I said to myself, "Please God, no! She is going to bug the shit out of me." But you already know there aren't any real accidents. Brenda Brockman was every bit of two hundred and fifty pounds, about five feet and two inches tall, with little beady brown eyes. She had a little turned-up nose, freckles, and long, dark, curly hair.

She asked, "How much is a reading?" with a nasally voice.

I usually charged one hundred dollars, but I purposely said five hundred so she would scram.

She asked "What can you do for fifty dollars?"

I was just about to tell her what I could do *to her* free, when something inside reminded me I was supposed to help people, so I gave her a quick read for fifty dollars. I sat her down and told her what I saw in the cards: family problems with her sisters.

"Oh my God! Yes! My two sisters are in therapy!"

I also saw an ex-husband, Rob, who wouldn't give her half of the equity for their house because she had inherited a million bucks.

"Oh my God, Regina you're amazing!" she said. "Rob has been giving me a very hard time."

Then I told her somebody named Mary is behind the house issue, that it wasn't just Rob.

"Oh my God! That's my-mother-in-law!"

Finally I said, "And you're nursing heartache. You have problems in love."

"Yes! Oh my God, Regina!! I've gone to other psychics, but they're not like you!"

She handed me two hundred dollars.

The next day, she sent Rob. I read for Rob and told him that I saw him letting go of Brenda's share of the equity in the house and letting go of the past. I told him his mother was asking for something purely for her own benefit that would stir up dissension in the long run. I saw that his mother had given them a little money to purchase the house years ago. Now she wanted that money back. He paid me two hundred and said it was from Brenda. The following day, Mary, the mother-in-law came. I saw immediately that she didn't like Brenda and wasn't going to step aside. I was cordial, gave her a quick read, and pleasantly sent her on her way. She never paid me.

I thought, *Well, that's that.* But a few minutes later, I heard Brenda jingling and clinking down the corridor of the mall again.

"I want to talk to you about the love problem I have now," she said.

It was lunchtime, and by now, I had a huge line of people waiting for readings, so I said, "Okay, but I'm busy right now; can you give me a couple of hours?"

"Sure."

She came back in ten minutes.

"I'm next!" she said, butting in line.

"Brenda, come back in a little while, please," I said. Her keys jabbed a little old lady, and her demeanor frightened some of the people.

"Okay. I'll be back."

She came back in five minutes.

"I'm *next*!"

"I can't see you right now! Wait a little bit."

She got frantic.

"I need *help* right now! I need the reading right now! I have all this money, and I *need your help*! I know you can help me! You're the only one who can help me! You're the real deal!"

Then, she turned to the line of clients, "This woman is awesome! She is so good! She caught on to everything in my life!"

Then back to me, "Please can I just come talk to you?"

I felt sorry for her. "Okay. Sit down for a minute, and let me at least finish this reading." I said, praying the other people in line wouldn't get pissed off. But they were very kind and gracious about it. Some had already paid for readings, so I rescheduled them for the next day.

Finally, I finished. She was so happy, the jingling sounded like sleigh bells, all the way to the chair.

"Okay, Brenda. What can I do for you?"

"Look, you have to listen to me!" she said handing me the picture of a cheesy-looking Puerto Rican dance hall stud. He had a mustache, slicked hair, his shirt unbuttoned down to the naval—the works.

"I want you to get this man for me! I don't care what it takes! Whatever you have to do!"

I told her it would not be easy. Brenda had a lot of anger.

"Brenda, you did lots of bad things to him. My guides are telling me you did something bad to his car. He is not happy. It cost him a lot of money to fix it. I see you are a very spiteful and jealous person."

Brenda told me what had happened. Carlos, the man she professed to love, was the Puerto Rican Salsa King. He taught salsa dancing at all the clubs in Kendall and South Miami, and he was always out clubbing. The night he and Brenda met, he was really, really drunk, and she had driven him home. They ended up having sex. She started going to his classes at Café Iguana, a popular dance club in South Miami. She was stalking him. He wanted nothing more to do with her. But he was compassionate, and he wasn't mean to her. He called her *Mi Muñeca,* which is Spanish for "my little doll." He was a real ladies' man, but that was it.

Brenda, however, wanted more—candles, decadent dinners, and lofty declarations of love. She went to Café Iguana and saw Carlos dancing with another girl, Isabel. She lost it. She went outside and poured battery acid all over the front end of his Camaro. Someone saw her do it, and they called the police right on the spot. To avoid jail, she said she had an alcohol addiction. They sent her to a drug and alcohol rehabilitation center, where she stayed a few weeks and then signed herself out.

As she told me these things, she also said she loved this man. She never asked me if they belonged together or if he loved her. She just asked, "Can you get him for me?"

I told her that if she loved him, she shouldn't do such things or display such abusive, dominant behavior.

But she didn't listen.

After our session, she went out and found Carlos at Café Iguana partying with his brother. Brenda insulted the man's brother, insulted his friends, and the girls they were with, finally coming on to Carlos, slapped him, called him a "stupid Spic slut," *then* told him all the *sexual* things she wanted to do to him, in front of the group.

"Brenda! You are obsessed. The only way I can get this man for you is a complete image renewal for you. It will cost fifty thousand dollars."

"What can you do for twenty-five thousand?"

This woman was going to force me to earn my money by ripping it out of my own throat. Brenda was determined to rub against the grain. No one could help a girl who wanted to wage a losing battle, with no regard for the outcome. Then I remembered the words of the preacher: "The question is, are you helping people?"

"Okay, Brenda. I'll knock off some money. But you have to do as I say!" I warned her.

She told me she had stopped working so she could focus on tailing him wherever he went. She bought him a brand new Toyota Supra, so he'd forgive her, which he refused. Then she bought him all this fancy jewelry and tickets to Colorado and Las Vegas, which he also refused.

"Go to Colorado by yourself. You need to clear your head. While you're there, I'll prepare a potion for you to help you make improvements in your demeanor," I said.

She went there by herself for a week, and I prepared the potion. While she was there, she became obsessive again. She couldn't go to the toilet without talking to me first. I stepped it up. Using one ounce of cherry brandy, one ounce of peach brandy, one teaspoon full of honey, and a sprinkling of cumin powder, I whipped up a tonic for inspiring love or passion. This I set aside in a tiny green bottle. Then, for renewed vision and intellect, I mixed one ounce of green mint cordial, two ounces of white gin, and one teaspoonful of white corn syrup. This I poured into a goatskin bag from Botanica Nena, a large Santeria supply depot in Little Havana. Fresh potions must only be contained in glass or goatskin bags, in order to preserve their potency. She drank both potions by a lake in her backyard, under a full moon. Three months later, she called me and asked if I had any information on Carlos yet.

I said, "Brenda, you're not ready. I still see Isabel around him. You're not working hard enough. He still thinks you're a fruitcake. The only way he'll give you a chance is if you show him you're somewhat normal. Words are extremely important. When people pick their phrases gently and sensitively, they can make even the most unsavory proposals seem acceptable. Harsh and thoughtless statements, like calling him 'stupid Spic' or 'Spic slut' create resentment and strife where none need exist."

She said, "I'd rather see him *dead* than with another woman!"

"Brenda, he teaches dance! He will always be dancing with other women. I need to meditate to find out why you are so sadistic when you're angry."

I uncovered through meditation that her father had been a Satan worshipper. She and her sisters were seeing therapists and hypnotists because their father, who had been part of a New Jersey–based cult, had committed acts of molestation on her and her sisters. She was already in

116

therapy for this and getting help through hypnosis and counseling, so I didn't think it was necessary to open up the wound again, but I knew it had a lot to do with her behavior. Though I knew the counseling and hypnosis were stirring up new emotions for her and starting the process of healing, it wasn't enough. She also needed a release from her past—a soul-clearing. I told her I'd be happy to perform this for twenty thousand dollars. But she didn't heed my advice. She left very upset. Later that night she came to my booth at the mall in a black lace dress that made her look like a stuffed sausage. She said she was going to see Carlos teach his classes that night.

I said, "I really, really wish you would not go out tonight. Leave him out of your fun this evening. Enjoy yourself. Then go home and leave him alone."

I knew that was not going to be the case. At 3:00 A.M. she called my house saying she saw the Salsa King dancing seductively with Isabel and a score of other women who had signed up for the course. She punched Isabel in the jaw, tore another woman's hair out, and was now downtown with the police. She wanted Romy to come down to the jail and bail her out. That's when I drew the line.

"You need to straighten out, Brenda! Quit using love as a crutch!"

She came to me the next day. Her ex-husband had bailed her out. Black eyeliner smeared, she was still in the same black lace outfit.

She said, "Okay. I'm ready to do whatever you say now."

I said, "No I'm sick of it."

"Please! Please! I want to be happy with him!"

I said, "No, Brenda. You had your chance for the soul-cleansing. You'd have to make major changes."

She left, cleaned up, and came back in a few hours in her leggings and keys. Clink-clink ca-clink-clink. In her arms she carried gifts for me: crystals from Montana, rose quartz, white quartz, and bloodstone. She said they were to help me regain the energy I lose with clients like her. I was touched by her gesture, caring for my health and wanting me to know she knew she was a drain. She bought me a gift certificate to Joe's Stone

Crab, my favorite restaurant. That was also thoughtful. She knew I was trying to have another baby, and she gave me an envelope calling it "baby fund" money. It contained five thousand dollars.

Finally, she gave me yet another envelope and said, "Look, I don't want the soul-clearing, but take the money. If you don't want it, give it to charity." It contained twenty thousand dollars. I softened. Unless people want to help themselves, even if they paid me a million bucks, I could never do anything for them. It's God's divine mercy. He sees how hard they're working to change and sets things right.

"Okay, Brenda, I'll work with you. But it's not about the money. Money doesn't give you the power to beat up people or befriend people. Money can't fix everything. You have kindness and goodness, and you need to let it show through. If you do that you can have Carlos. I see *he will love you*, if you show him your kindness."

I prayed over her and had her ask forgiveness from her heart. Then we began the weeklong soul-clearing. First, I had her sleep in a white cloth, naked, with some fresh herbs that would absorb all the impurity out of her heart and mind. Then we took a bunch of markers and wrote words on the cloth. We wrote the words "depression, sadness, low self-esteem, heartbreak, anxiety, and confusion." We wrapped her up naked in it on the top of a hill and had her unroll herself all the way down the hill. Finally, we went thirty miles out to Jones Beach on Key Biscayne, burned it, and never looked back.

Every day for three months, I had lunch and dinner with this woman. I was making sure she was really dedicated to ridding herself of the anger. She stopped clubbing and drinking. That's not an easy thing to do in Miami, when you've been in and out of bars every night, by yourself, driving home plastered drunk. After three months, I let her go clubbing, again, by herself. But she did not get drunk. She looked all over for Carlos, but he had stopped teaching at any club where he might run into her. She drove from club to club, looking for him, and finally found him in a small Latino bar south of Coral Reef. She showed up, just as he was finishing a private class.

He said, "Are you sick and crazy? I can't believe you've found me! I can't believe you're here!" He started laughing.

Then he said, "Why are you crazy about me Brenda? I've never seen anyone so driven! What do you want, Brenda? We only had *one night* together. I see you everywhere, and you're always looking at me. You're always looking to hurt me, and you beat up my girlfriend!"

She said, "Oh? Is that your girlfriend?"

He said, "Not anymore. I have a *stalker*. My family thinks you're crazy, and they all know I have a stalker—one that's looking to kill me."

She took a deep breath and recited the speech I had given her.

"Carlos, I'm in love with you, deeply. It's a fact I can't change. It comes from within, for no explainable reason, other than God put it in my heart. I have been going through some hard times because of some issues I've had in the past, but I'm healing now. And though I have been insanely jealous, I understand you are a dance teacher and have every right to dance with many women. I'm just trying to tell you I'm sorry. I respect your work. I promise it will never happen again."

Then my magic happened. They ended up drinking together and laughing about all the crazy stunts she'd pulled to try to get his attention. After a few hours of laughing and getting to know each other all over again, she drove him back to her house where they made love all night, sexily, slowly, and softly.

The next morning, he woke up and said, "Let's go to Key West, *Muñeca*!" She called me at 10:00 A.M.

"You did it! Regina, you did it! I said everything you told me to say and after the soul-clearing and total image renewal, I've felt much, much better. And you know what? I really, really mean it!! He's in my bedroom right now! I'm making him breakfast, and he wants to go to Key West. Just the two of us."

"That's wonderful, Brenda! Now remember: *Be nice!*"

"I will! I promise! I love you, Regina! Thanks for all your help!"

A few months later, I heard the keys. Clink-clink, ca-clink-clink. They

119

came by my booth, together, and said they were opening up a cellular phone place. Brenda had a ring on her left hand and new black leggings.

"Is this what I think it is?" I asked, grinning.

"We're getting married in the Keys this spring. We'd love for you to be there!"

"Thank you. I hope I'll be available!"

Sometimes clients call me and complain, saying, "What you predicted didn't happen!" But they're wrong. What I predict, meaning what my guides tell me or show me, happens. Ultimately, the clients see the wisdom in doing what is asked of them. Whatever spells I conjure, *the magic* has to come from them.

TWELVE

Missing Canary

As my bank account grew, so did my head. Romy and I hadn't been getting along. The relationship had grown stale. I often thought about leaving Romy and getting a fresh start with the kids.

Then one day, Romy surprised me with a three-carat canary diamond. He bought it from some jeweler at The Exchange who dealt with a lot of mafiosos from Hollywood. It was brilliant cut, deeper than it was wide, the shade of lemon sorbet—beautiful.

Across time, Gypsies have associated the diamond with magic properties, healing, protection, and poisoning. The word *diamond* actually comes from the Greek word *adamao,* which means "I tame." I loved that ring so much it hurt. Romy knew how to get to me, and a diamond like that was the right size and weight to anchor my ass at home. I was tamed, too.

Oddly enough, about a month later, I got a call from a sweet little old lady. Guess what she'd lost?

"I don't really want a readin', but I'll pay you whatever it costs to sit with you," she said on the phone.

I said, "Fine. Come on down to my office."

Her sweet, Southern accent was appealing. "Can you help me find something?"

"A psychic can help find something only if the person or item is recently lost, like within three days. You're going to have to come in," I said.

"It says in your ad that you help find missing people," she said.

"Yes. Have you lost someone?"

"Well, I need to explain it to you."

"Okay, come down. If it's a person, you need to bring a picture."

"Awllright, honey."

A little later I heard my doorbells tinkling, and in walked this old lady with a yellow cigarette holder wearing a yellow turban, yellow shoes, and yellow bangles. It was meant only as a frame for her deeply plunging neckline accentuating her generous bosom. Punctuating her cleavage like the dot under an exclamation point was the most tremendous diamond brooch I'd ever seen. Then I noticed she was dripping in diamonds, from her wrists, ears, and neck. To make matters more comical, she had smeared a chic shade of magenta on her cheeks and lips, but it was too dark and ran over her lip line.

"What a lovely place you have."

"Thank you," I said.

"My name is Audrey," she said.

"It's a pleasure to meet you, Audrey. Please, sit down."

She sat across me while I spread the cards out on my desk. She sat with her back very straight and her tiny hands folded one on top of the other in her lap. Her perfume was one of those sticky, heavy, sweet scents old ladies use, like Chanel No. 5.

I took in her energy, her whole aura. I saw she was a giver and very wealthy, from old money. She had blue blood manners and Southern charm; she kept calling me "dahlin" and "honey."

"I kept your ad for three days. I saw it in the *Gazette*, and I kept it with me for three days," she said, as if announcing some big secret.

"Tell me, what made you decide to call my number?"

"Well, dear, I lost something very dear to my heart," she said.

"Okay, then, I'm going to close my eyes and contact the spirit around you and you're going to tell me what you lost and I'm going to see if I we can psychically find it."

I put my fingers on my temples and closed my eyes. They like that, the clients. It makes them feel like I'm concentrating intensely. Really, a true psychic need only ask their spirit guide for clarity, but anyway, you know the drama is part of the deal.

I said, "Audrey, I want you now to focus on what you lost and tell me what you lost."

"I lost . . . I lost an eight-carat canary yellow diamond."

My jaw dropped. My eyes popped open. She was still concentrating. I nearly died. I thought, *Who could lose an eight-carat diamond?* vowing to check my safe as soon as I got home. Then, a flash of green appeared in my head.

"I used to keep it on this finger right here," and she stuck up a bony marriage finger.

I saw it was not a wedding ring. Sentimental value, yes, but not her wedding ring.

"How can you lose an eight-carat diamond of any kind? Never mind. I'm seeing lots of green, something green. It's surrounded by green," I said.

"Yes dahlin'. It was with my emeralds. You see honey, I had a party at my estate. Nothing too fancy, some old friends and a few politicians. We had a pianist, and a beautiful ice sculpture by an artist from Bonnet House. It was lovely. But it went on to the wee hours of the night. I thought I put the diamond back in the safe after the party. I guess I had a little too much champagne. I must have put it on my nightstand because the next day, when I went to look for it, it was gone. I looked in the vault, behind the nightstand, under the bed, everywhere, but I couldn't find it. It wasn't anywhere; it was gone."

"Who else was there with you?' "

"Well, the maid. She comes in every morning to give me my medicine. But she's been my maid for twenty years, and I trust her with my life."

I said, "Well, okay. Was there anybody else in the room?"

"Oh no dahlin'. That room is locked when I'm not occupying it."

"Okay. Tell me the maid's name," I said.

"Her name is Margaret."

"Margaret?" I couldn't get a feeling from that name.

"Well, Margarite, Marguerite, like that. She's from El Salvador. My son lives with me, and we trust her with everything."

I said, "Okay."

She said, "You're seeing green because it was with my emeralds."

"Hmm . . ."

"It had to have been with my emeralds; I wore them that night, too; dahlin' that must be it. It was something that belonged to my grandmother, who was very, very dear to me." I could tell that she was telling the truth.

"Uh-huh. Tell me, when did you have it last?"

"I don't remember, honey. My memory's not what it used to be I'm afraid."

"Okay, I'm going to tell you. The maid had something to do with its disappearance."

"Oh my heavens, no!!"

"Yes, I think the maid took it," I said. "She took it, but it's still there."

"Oh no! What should I do?"

"Did you question her?"

"No."

"Maybe you should," I said.

"Oh my lord! Should I go check in her room and her things? See if she has it? My heavens!! Why would she do such a thing?"

I thought, *My God, you poor innocent soul.* She seemed so good, so righteous, that she could never, ever imagine anyone doing that to her.

"You need to go home, talk to her, and see her reaction. Have the house dusted for prints to scare her. Maybe she'll confess," I suggested.

"I guess I can do that. I guess I'll stop searching the house. But if I prove it was her, how am I supposed to let her go? I suppose this is God's way of telling me, if I have to lose something, I'm glad it's just a ring and nothing else."

"I know the ring is there. It's definitely there," I said. "I can see it and feel it there."

"Well, do you see anything else missing?"

"I feel things are about to start missing," I said.

She was devastated. It was too much for her to accept. I wanted to hug her and tell her it would be all right. She really didn't want to know anything else bad about Marguerite.

"Well, thank you for seeing me." She handed me five hundred dollars and got up. She looked so sad, like she now knew something she never wanted to know.

A few weeks later, she sent her friend to see me: another little old lady, well-dressed and polite, with some heavy, gold charm bracelets. She wasn't wearing a turban or anything dramatic. She wore no makeup and smelled like dry cleaning.

I said, "So, I understand Audrey is your neighbor?"

"Neighbor and best friend," she said. "I've known Audrey all my life. We've always been best friends. I know everything about Audrey, and she knows everything about me."

"What can I do for you?"

"Well, my name is Margie. I want to know if I'm goin' to meet a nice man soon. I'm real lonely in this big ole' house. I don't have any children, like Audrey does, or a pet—nothing. And I would like to meet someone real nice. Do you see me meeting someone nice over the summer?"

"Well, let's find out," I said.

I closed my eyes and put my fingers on my temples, and, voila! I saw this lady had been all over the house that night looking through Audrey's things and going through Audrey's closet and drawers.

"Margie," I said. "Is there anyone in particular you want me to focus on?"

"Well, I did meet a man the night of the party, but I don't know if he is a nice man. He is very attractive. He was very charming, but I don't know if he was sincere."

"Margie, are you sincere?" I asked.

"I most certainly am! What kind of question are you asking me? I am an absolutely decent person! I don't believe I can continue this readin'," she said.

"I'm sorry if I offended you, Margie. Let's continue, please. I will try again."

So I closed my eyes and told her to close hers as well and really focus on her loneliness: going to bed at night alone, eating alone, traveling alone. But I still kept seeing her rummaging through Audrey's things and nothing more. The guides would not reveal anything else.

"Okay, Margie, are you sure you're thinking about what I told you?"

"Yes, Regina. I'm thinking exactly about my loneliness. Why? Are you not seeing anyone out there for me?"

"Let's give it some time, Margie. Sometimes my third eye doesn't work as fast as a computer. Let me try something else," I said, and I gave her a cleansing bath potion and told her to come back the next day.

The next afternoon, she returned, pissed off because I hadn't foretold a new lover, but I still had charged her. I didn't think she'd get upset paying for the consultation, but you know everyone wants something free. She got my special cleansing bath potion, which you can't buy in a store. I make it fresh every morning with goat's milk and hard-to-find herbs. I drive into Hialeah every morning to get the stock for the day. Every night I throw it away because its potency has expired. Anyway, she returned angry and stiff.

"I did what you said, and quite frankly, this bath is horrid. It smells like fish," Margie said.

"Yes, it's not really made to beautify the skin. I agree. But it certainly opens up the airways for the guides."

"Well, I have a question," she said, indignantly.

"Yes, I'm sure you have lots of them. Let's start with the reading, though, because I'm fresh from meditation, and I bet I can answer most of them right now."

She just sat there with a big sourpuss face. The phone rang, and it was Audrey.

"Hello?"

"Yes, honey, it's me, Audrey. I'm awfully sorry to bother you at work, but it seems we have a bit of a situation here. Well, I think I may need you to make a house call. Do you do that? Can you come to my house, dear?"

"Normally I don't."

"I'll pay you two thousand dollars, dear; I know it is a great imposition to you."

"I can come over," I said, careful not to give away who was on the phone to Margie. "I have a client here at the moment, but I'll drive over right afterward. I'll call you for directions when I'm in the car. You live over in Parkland? Don't you?"

"Yes, dahlin'; I hate to be an inconvenience to you, but I really need you to come now."

She was firm, not hysterical, but I could tell this was about more than a ring.

"Okay, I'll be there soon." I hung up.

"Margie, I am so sorry I cannot complete our session today, but I am going to give you a refund and reschedule with you for tomorrow morning. Would that suit you? I really want you to be happy, and I have so much to tell you, but there's been an emergency I must respond to right now."

"I don't know what kahnd of business you're runnin'. I think you're just stringin' me along to keep me coming back. I don't think you have anything to tell me, and furthermore, I don't believe you have any fortune-telling abilities whatsoever. I think you're also foolin' my friend Audrey, and when she finds out what you just did to me, you won't be able to take any more money from her, either. She's less of a pushover than I am!"

"I'm sorry you feel that way," I said to her, ushering her out the door. "I really would like to see you again, but I understand if this emergency has made you doubtful. Please call me if you change your mind." I showed her out and tore for the car.

As I was driving to Audrey's, I kept getting the picture of the ring laying in the green—surrounded by green. And I kept seeing Margie running her hands on top of clothes in a drawer. She was inside and outside and searched through some shopping bags in the back of Audrey's closet.

When I arrived, Marguerite, dressed in a big white T-shirt and pants, was bringing in the mail. She looked like she was in her early forties. To me, she looked like Bianca Jagger—square jaw, dark wavy hair. Except for her protruding belly, I would say she had a nice body. I drove past her and parked in front of the house on the circular drive. Audrey answered the door in a black turban and matching pantsuit.

"Thank you for coming, dear. Please, follow me," she said, giving me a short hug.

"What's going on, Audrey? What happened?" I said.

"I want you to talk to Marguerite, before I say anything to her. Just to make sure."

"To make sure she took it?" I asked.

"Yes."

"Audrey, I know she took it. My guides have shown me. Now, if you want me to look at her, to see where she's hidden it, that's fine. Bring her to me. But I can assure you it's not in the house."

"Oh no! No! No dear! You'll have to take a peek at her while she's in the kitchen. I don't generally introduce my maid to my guests. She'll suspect something. Go into the kitchen. It's just over there," she said waving me in the direction with a long bony finger.

"Pretend you got lost on your way to the powder room and ask her for directions. Sweetly, now. Then take a good, long look at her and tell me what you think, honey. I trust you," she said.

I walked past some open French doors from which a fresh, warm summer breeze blew. I edged closer, and I saw Audrey's huge, lush green lawn, exactly like the one I had seen in my vision. Beyond it was a lake with a beautiful white gazebo next to it. My gut told me that looking at Marguerite was not important at this time.

So I walked outside and looked for the ring up and down in the grass. I walked really slow all the way to the gazebo at the edge of the lake, heels sinking all the way. But I couldn't find it.

The lawn was so squishy from all the rain we'd been having, I gave up on the Gucci heels and took them off. The house was gorgeous from way out there. The lake was so calm, I thought, *Her parties must be beautiful out by the gazebo*, and sank down on a bench.

It was quite serene, and I fell into meditation, calling for my spirit guides to speak to me. Suddenly, they revealed it to me. It was lying right next to the gazebo the whole time, face down and half buried, all but the shank, surrounded by the green, green grass. It was amazing—huge and even more yellow than mine!! I put it on my finger so I wouldn't lose it and lusted after it uncontrollably.

"Better check and see if it's cursed," I thought after catching myself putting it in my pocket! I ran back to the house with the ring and saw Marguerite watching from a window. She looked furious.

Nevertheless, I called out to Audrey, "Audrey! Audrey! I found the ring!"

"What? Oh m'gosh! Bless your heart! Bless you, Regina! How am I ever going to repay you for finding my grandmother's ring?!

"Audrey I have to tell you what I saw in meditation out there in your gazebo. Marguerite took it and lost it. She hasn't been looking for it with you; she's been looking for it on her own. So has your friend Margie. I'm gonna do another meditation on you to figure this out. I'm not a psychic detective, Audrey, but this is not the end of this problem. You are going to lose something much bigger than this. But its identity has not yet been revealed."

Driving home in the Benz, I thought, *That maid was too hot and sexy to be just a regular, standard issue maid.* Something had kept her from leaving and building a life of her own with her own man and her own house. There was some kind of affair going on, I could feel it. I could hear secrets and whispers in my ears.

I parked, went into my little prayer room, and meditated, and before I even finished, I got another call.

"Regina, honey?"

"Hello Audrey! Listen I want to ask you something. Do you have any children?"

"Well, that's just what I want to ask you about. My son said he is going to buy some property in El Salvador. It's a rather large bit of land with some oil wells and a beer-bottling plant. And I wanted to know if this is a good investment. He just told me. He wants what's left of his trust, and then he wants me to join the venture, sell some of our other investments, and be his silent partner. Regina, I just don't know if this is a wise thing. But Marguerite said he knows what he's doing, dahlin', and well, could you do a readin' on that for me, dear?"

"Audrey, do not give your son any money. And don't ask your maid anything else about him."

"Why dear?"

"I'll tell you after I meditate on this. And please don't confide in Margie, either, Audrey. Just keep to yourself for a little while, okay?" But of course, Audrey couldn't trust me because I am a psychic whom she barely knew. I knew she went and confronted her son.

I meditated on her ring, the friend, the maid, and her son, and all I got was that she was definitely going to get scammed by two of them. I felt Margie was broke. I now clearly saw the maid and Audrey's son were indeed having an affair. In fact, they had carried on, passionately, for many, many, years.

I tried to call Audrey three times that afternoon, but got Marguerite instead, who said she'd gone out. The next day I tried Audrey again. Again, Marguerite fed me some bullshit and took a message. This cat and mouse went on for another day, and I gave up. Clients are notorious for wanting my attention intensely for a few months and then disappearing. So I gave up.

Three months later, I got a call from Margie.

"Regina? This is Margie, Audrey's friend. I wondered if you have time for the readin' now? I want to find out about a man I met at a luncheon. I'll pay you for the whole afternoon, and money is no object. I don't want any interruptions this time. I have so many questions. Oh! And I heard you found Audrey's big ole' ring. That was sure clever, girl!"

"Thank you, Margie. My guides found it. Come in whenever you like. By the way, I haven't heard from Audrey. How is she doing?"

"Oh, well, of course I expect you haven't heard. Audrey died—terrible tragedy. Everyone is very upset."

"Oh my God! How did she die?"

"Heart attack, dear. Then she fell and bashed her head in on the patio steps. It was a horrible, horrible accident."

"Where's her son, Margie?"

"He's in El Salvador, on business. Can I come by this afternoon, honey?"

"Yes, that's fine. Tell me, Margie, what happened to the maid?"

"Who? Marguerite? She's gone, dear. She went back to her homeland."

"Back to . . . ?"

"Back to El Salvador. She's from El Salvador. The house is on the market. There's no more work for her here, and she wanted to have her baby with her family close by."

"Baby?!"

"Yes, dear, Marguerite was pregnant. Didn't Audrey tell you? I would like to stop by to sit with you around 2:00 P.M. Now I met a nice man at a luncheon, and he's a little older than me, but a real Southern gentleman. . . ."

THIRTEEN

Cyber Secrets

The rich old biddies from Parkland made such interesting clients (murder; conspiracy; hot, pregnant maids) that I decided to move my office closer to it, at the tip of the Everglades, in a small town called Reston.

Reston, at the time, was known for being a family-oriented community. It was landscaped by Vidarva, the same company that designed the signature look for all the Mutton Mouse amusement parks. Many professional athletes built huge estates in some of the more upscale developments, reserved for the elite of Miami in flight from the crime wave afflicting some of its more affluent areas.

The whole town was extraordinarily tranquil: dads coaching Little League, moms in the PTA, kids in Boy Scouts. It was immaculate—freshly painted mailboxes, neatly trimmed shrubs, and lots and lots of sprinklers. You could set your watch by the sprinklers.

I opened a nice little boutique office in a strip mall, next to a Spanish *tapas* bar and a nail salon. Before I had a chance to hang up my neon sign, a woman walked into my boutique in a panic. I felt a very warm presence with her—a spirit guiding her.

"Can I help you?" I said.

"I come becows I need to ask you something. I have problem wit my doter. I want to know why did she do dis terribel ting?"

"What terrible thing? Sit down. Please, sit down. And relax," I added.

The woman burst into tears.

"I don' speak very good Eenglish. I am from Nicaragua. I came here seven years ago. I came to work to house cleaning. I do house cleaning six days a week. I go to two houses a day. I work bery hard. I have many houses. One lady name is Miss Tiffany Crysp. I bring my doter here last year; finally I haf money to bring her. She is bery beeutiful. I love my doter, and I want a good life for her, here in this country. An' she come to live wit' me last year. She does not have a green card. I clean this house an' my doter baby-sitting for Miss Tiffany.

"One day I go to Miss Tiffany's house, and she tell me to look on de computadora. She say my doter is on the computadora. She say her husband find it, by accidente. I look at the computadora, and she is there with no clothes on! She is doing dis bad ting! Bery bad! I need you help me!! Please! *Por favor! Por el amor de Dios!* Please!"

"What was she doing?"

"She . . . she . . . she . . . has no clothes on . . . and she was doing de porno!"

"*What*? How old is your daughter?"

"Fifteen."

"Oh my God! What site?"

"What?"

"What site? What is the Internet address, so I can look her up and concentrate on her image?

The woman looked at me blankly.

"Never mind, who told you to look on the computadora?"

"Miss Tiffany Crysp, in Reston."

"Okay, so where is your daughter now?"

"Home, *en la casa*. She don't know I know. I gonna tell her I know, and I gonna send her back to Nicaragua. I no bring her here to do dis! She gotta go back!!"

"I am so sorry to hear this, Miss, uh . . . ?"

"My name ees Gloria. My doter name is Rosa."

"Gloria, I am so sorry to hear this. Let's look into this. Please come sit down. Let me get my tarot out. Just relax, get comfortable, and focus on your daughter."

"Who do dis?"

I told her what I saw in the cards. There was a tall, dark, older man. Much older than Rosa and very distinguished, gray hair around the temples, and a small chin. He looked like he drove an expensive silver car. I asked her if she knew anyone like that.

"My doter has a boyfren'. He looks like dat, and I no like him."

"I don't like him either, Gloria. He is involved in this. Don't let her out with this man anymore. Bring her to me tomorrow or whenever you can; I know you're very busy. God bless you, and don't worry. I will find out how to help her."

"*Ay gracias!!* Tank you. Tank you bery much! *Muchas gracias, señora! Muy amable.* I pay you now?"

"No! Don't pay me. Free. *Gratis.* I want to help you," I said. This poor woman and her daughter were obviously victims of sex trafficking. Kids caught up in this are usually younger than Rosa. When a husband gets busted watching porn on the Internet, he comes clean. So the need that fuels the market may also have a hand in stopping it. I believe God sometimes chooses to make it obvious that He has stepped in and made a way where there seems to be no way. And I don't charge God.

The next day, Gloria came in with Rosa, and she was stunning: long, wavy hair, curvy hips, cinnamon skin, with freckles across her nose and cheeks. I opened the tarot and began to read for her, while her mother translated. I saw that in four to six years, she was supposed to become a teacher and a mother. I also saw that she really didn't want to be around this bad man and that she was deeply ashamed.

"Why did you do this?" I asked her.

"*Porque hiciste esto?!*" her mother said.

She said this guy had approached her and a friend one day after school at the apartment complex they lived in, on the outskirts of Reston. He asked them if they wanted a job, and they'd hesitantly said yes. He told them not to be scared because he was a prominent Miami business-man who needed models for his magazine.

He said they'd be paid, and fed, on-site. They didn't need green cards. The next day they skipped school, and he picked them up in his Jaguar and took them to a Doral warehouse to "model." The entire job consisted of meeting all his "partners" and sitting on their laps. Rosa said they plied her and her friend with wine and started fondling them, taking turns with each of them. Soon, she said, the guy took her into another room. No sooner did she lie on the bed than she passed out. She could not remember what happened next. All she knew was that she and her friend were taken home later, groggy and tired, and he paid each of them fifty dollars.

Later that week, he called Rosa and asked her out on a date. He took Rosa for a nice dinner and brought her home. He asked that she not tell anyone they were now "dating" because she was so young and he could get into trouble in this country. He told her he cared for her and would take care of her and her mother. Then he gave her one hundred dollars.

Soon, Rosa said, he asked to be introduced to a bunch of her girl-friends. For every girlfriend who would "model" for him, Rosa got ten dollars. Every time she "posed for the magazine," she got fifteen dollars. She said she did it for the money because she wanted to help her mother. Then they both fell apart.

The afternoon Miss Tiffany showed her fifty-dollar-a-day maid, Glo-ria, that her daughter was naked, spread-eagle on a porn site, she had also fired her. When they were leaving, I pulled Gloria aside and asked her what she was going to do. She said she was going to send Rosa back to Nicaragua for sure.

I said, "Good. I'm going to put a protective shield on you and your daughter. Leave me your address, in case I want to mail something to you." After they left, I called information and contacted Tiffany Crysp.

"Hello, my name is Regina Milbourne. May I speak to Miss Tiffany Crysp?"

"This is Tiff!!!" she said, in her perky, strained voice.

"Hi, Ms. Crysp. I'm a master psychic, and I have an office right here in Reston. I'm just calling residents to offer them free readings for a trial run. Have you ever had a psychic reading?"

"No! Wow!"

"Would you be interested in learning what exciting adventures lie in your near future?"

"Wow! Yes! I think that would be neat!"

"Great! Well, why don't you tell me what time you're free tomorrow, and we'll set up a psychic reading for you, completely free of charge."

"Well, let's see . . . I drop off Rowyn by 7, and then Devon's in by 8 . . . oh . . . then I have to pick up the dry cleaning, cause if I don't do it then, I'll forget . . . Oh! And I have tennis at 10, and, uh, well, what time did you say I should come in?"

"Come in at 11:00 A.M. My office opens at 11:00 A.M."

"Great! See you then, and thanks!"

The next day she was already waiting in front of the store when I drove up, in her little T-shirt, capri pants, and Louis Vuitton purse—the Reston Mommy uniform. She had a perky little face, turned-up button nose, and a fresh-cut blonde Jennifer Aniston hairdo.

"Hi! Oh Hi! How are you! Are you the Reston psychic?" she gushed, shaking my hand.

"Yep! That's me. Why don't you come in and let me put my things away in the back. Can I offer you a cup of tea?"

"No thanks! Wow! Your place is real pretty! I've never been inside a psychic store before! Is this how they all look? With this beautiful furniture . . . is that a mahogany desk? Oh wow! You even have herbal baths!" she said browsing through my potions.

"Well, not all look the same. My decorator said I have an 'eclectic' style. I make fresh batches of that bath every morning for a week, one week out of every month, so what you see there is fresh out of the goat's udder. It's a cleansing bath. So, have you got some questions ready?"

"Now this is a free reading, right? You know I've always believed in psychics, but I never had the opportunity to go to a really good one. I went to one a long time ago, and she told me I would marry a blond man and have two children. And she was right. So, let's see if you're really good! I really don't have any questions."

"I can tell you what lies in your future just by reading the cards. And yes, this is absolutely free. Sit down now, and we'll begin. Close your eyes, and focus on what you want to know and find out. Make three wishes, and I'm going to shuffle the cards."

"Okay."

"Okay, now tell me when to stop shuffling."

"Stop!"

"Okay, Tiffany, now open your eyes and cut the cards from left to right with your right hand. Good, good. Now pick a pile. Good. Okay! Let's see what the guides can tell you about your exciting future."

"This is so neat!"

"Oh. Oh my . . ."

"What? What?" she asked, anxiously.

"Well, let me check something, hold on, now . . ."

"Oh God! Is it bad? Oh I knew it! I knew I wouldn't get a good reading. This figures."

"Well, now, hold on. Hold on, Tiffany. It isn't that bad. Your kids are fine. Your husband has a little problem. Well, it's a big problem. Uh, what's this porno stuff?"

"Oh my God! Do the *cards* show that? Where? *How do you know that*?"

"Tiffany, the cards are telling me you have a lot of porn in your house—the kind that could get someone arrested. Your husband has a problem—a big problem, Tiffany. He's spent thousands of dollars on illegal Internet child porn, and he's not going to stop on his own."

Tiffany burst into tears.

"Tiffany, listen to me; we can help him, but it's going to cost some money," I said, casually baiting the hook.

"How? How can I help him?"

"We need to do a cleansing. We need to find all the names of all the sites he visits, all the images he's downloaded, all the filth he's got and get rid of it all. You need to bring me his hard drive. Then we're going to cleanse him, pray over him, and do a little magic, so he'll stay away from the porn. The whole thing's going to cost around fifteen thousand. I know you would do anything to help him. If you don't, you'll lose your house, your cars, your country club membership . . ." I just tossed the line in gently, wiggled it around a bit—teased the fish.

"*Stop*! I don't want to hear anymore! I get it! Okay, look, I barely know you. How do I know this will work?"

"Tiffany. You said it yourself. I *barely* know you. But I know your husband masturbates about a hundred times a day to pictures of little kids. It's the only thing that gets him off. You know this," I said, looking her directly in the eye.

"I don't care to hear that kind of talk."

I picked up the cards and put them away.

"I may be a lot of things, but I'm never wrong."

"You really need the hard drive?"

"Yes. It's the only way. You see, when you ask him to delete things or get rid of things, he just hides it from you. You need to cleanse him because we can't start any other type of healing work until he is cleansed."

"I understand. But fifteen thousand is too much money."

"Well, you don't have to decide right now. If you decide to let me help you, you know where I can be reached," I said, standing and showing her to the door. "I'm sorry it couldn't have been better news."

"Do I have to pay it all at once?" she asked.

"No, of course not. I can take three installments of five thousand dollars. Give me five thousand right now, and I can get started on his cleansing lotion. It's a massage lotion men love because it feels so good to have it rubbed on. You rub it all over his chest and his legs. It has no smell, and it provides a little relaxation. Then you bring the hard drive with the second five thousand and bring the rest when it comes time to pick it up again. And try to schedule it during the day, when he's away at work."

She left and came back with five thousand dollars. She handed it to me and walked out, without so much as a good-bye. The reality of her situation had hit home.

At noon the next day, Tiffany came to my store with the hard drive.

"I have to have this back by six o'clock. And here's your money."

"Thank you. And here is your cleansing lotion. This should be rubbed on him every day for seven days, right before he goes to bed," I said, taking the hard drive to the back of the boutique.

"Okay, I'll try it. I get my money back if it doesn't work, right?"

"You'll get everything," I said.

As soon as she pulled away, I took the hard drive to the *Baro's* house. He was eating lunch.

"What's this for, Gina?" he said still chewing, a napkin tied around his neck.

"Child pornography," I said. "Take it to your guy in the Broward sheriff's office. Here's the name and address of the guy who owns this. This guy," I said, patting the computer, "is not running the ring."

"Crazy people in this world. *Disgusting*. I heard a story today on the news about a guy who used himself as a human ziplock baggie," he said.

"What?"

"Yeah, this poor guy, twenty-three-year-old Colombian, allowed the warlords to open up his thigh and place three condoms of coke inside it. After they sewed him up, he boarded a plane. When he landed, he was supposed to just get off the plane and meet up with the dealers who would extract the 'shipment' from his thigh and sew him back up."

"Oh my God! That's horrible!!"

"Yeah. Anyways, he never made it. One of the condoms burst right after the plane landed. By the time he got to his check point, he was a goner. They dumped his body in a canal off the Tamiami trail. Some people will do anything for money," he sighed.

"I would reverse that. Some people with money will do anything— including trying to buy other people."

"You did good, Gina."

Tiffany never came back to pick up the computer. A few weeks later, the little strip mall was hopping as I pulled in. The doors of the nail salon were wide open, and you could hear loud, raucous laughter coming from inside. The *tapas* bar was also unusually busy for a lunch crowd. Alberto, the owner, came running out grinning, as I got out of my Bentley.

"Did you see the news? Some guys in Reston were arrested for running a kiddie porn ring! Most of the chicks in it were daughters of maids from over in the Windmill Plains Estates! They're on the news right now! Come in here and watch this!"

Later that afternoon, Gloria thanked me for the ten thousand dollars in person with a basket of crispy empanadas and plenty of tears.

"You don' know how much you halp me an my doter! Eres un angel! You are an angel! Now chee don feel like trash. I bring her back! Chee go to escool in Broward Community College to become a teacher jus' like you say! Chee is bery happy! An I am so grateful, Miss Regina! I don' know how to tank you!"

"Gloria, God sees how hard you work and how much you try. He told me to help you. Don't thank me, thank God. Keep praying. He hears every word you say," I said, giving her a hug.

"By the way, who died last year?" I asked her.

"Ah, my mother die. But how you know, Miss Regina?"

"Because she's with you, watching over you. You're not alone, Gloria."

FOURTEEN

Mere

swear in the name of Jesus, if you ever have to deal with voodoo, run the other way. It will suck the life out of you! Even if you triumph over it, you lose so much your life is never the same. True psychics, like *moi*, dumb enough to take it on, often feel the force of voodoo faith. But hindsight is 20/20, as they say.

The very name *Haiti* conjures images of voodoo priests, zombies, and insidious dictators. A hybrid of French traditions and African beliefs produced a unique culture quite unlike any other in the world. Ships in eighteenth and nineteenth centuries crammed with West African Yoruba people bound for the Isle of Hispaniola brought with them the Vodun religion. Its roots may go back more than six thousand years in Africa. However, Haitian deities have a more sinister edge than their African counterparts. The French capitalized on voodoo fear to keep the Africans as slaves. Slaves used Vodun to confuse the French and conceal crimes from them. Fifty thousand Haitian refugees fled Haiti in the 1990s due to political turmoil and landed here, in Miami. Miami is truly North America's Voodoo Central.

Haitians who practice voodoo don't hide like Gypsies. They are a subculture among us. They're too busy struggling, coupling, and conjuring. For years, psychics and voodoiennes have fed off one another in a way that has kept all our families well-dressed and warm. But unlike psychics, these Haitians live their voodoo. It is the strongest type of magic in the world. It is their true religion, pure and simple. All forms of sorcery, black and white, are not just practiced, but worshipped. The priests of the society work as a unit to master the system. Their schooling includes everything, even necromancy. They feel they've got to create the bad mojo of the world to learn how to undo it.

My brush with voodoo started off innocently enough. One day, a client of mine called me and said, "I want you to come and read for my girlfriend. She's having a big birthday party, and she wants you to do readings for all her guests, too."

I got dressed up, really fancy; the address was chi-chi. When I arrived, the bellman told me to go up on the private elevator, as Mrs. Bonner was expecting me. A tall, slim, supersophisticated, lady opened the door. I saw her top-of-the-line kitchen, her sixty thousand dollar marble floors, and furniture from the famous Design Center of the Americas. Music was playing softly, and she spoke with a French accent. Immediately, I saw she had had voodoo hands on her.

She said, "It's very nice to meet you. I'm Clotaire Bonner."

She invited me in. Her bartender poured me a glass of Krug champagne. She went to trim some flowers and began making floral arrangements.

"Where would you be most comfortable?" she asked.

I said, "I just need a small room off to the side." She took me into her library.

She said, "I really want you to spend as much time as you need with the women, and money is no object."

"Fine—I charge three hundred dollars per person."

Twenty people came to the party, all women—all catty. The party went on outside, on a balcony, and in the living room. She would bring the women to me one by one. I read for all the women at the party, and I could tell none of them liked her. In fact, they all hated her. They were jealous of her and horribly prejudiced. They had no room for a rich, Haitian woman. It made *me* sad. Only her friend Lucy, who was also my client, liked her.

Near the end of the party, it was Clotaire's turn for a reading, and I told her right off the bat that her mother was around her.

"You didn't even know her, but your mother is the cause of every problem you have ever had and will have, if you don't take her on," I said.

Then I told her there was white man in her life, and he was very prominent, but he hadn't been very good to her as of late.

"Yes, yes, I see," she said. "What about my ex?"

"He's all right. He misses you, but he will never come back. He is convinced you have sexual issues. That you are sexually dysfunctional," I said.

"You're right! You're right! I'm so ashamed, but I never, ever had an orgasm. I don't feel anything in my vagina. I never have. It's dead. I wish I were dead." She was very drunk by this time.

"Listen to me, Clotaire. There will be another man in your life, but you have to get rid of the handyman you're seeing now to be ready. The white handyman doesn't love you. He is sleeping with your good friend Suzanne, too."

"How on earth? My God, I knew it."

"If you stay with him, you will lose everything you worked so hard for. You need to rid yourself of him ASAP! There's going to be a foreign man. You're going to be traveling for your own enjoyment, and that's where you'll meet him. He has very light eyes. He is *gorgeous*! He has a very strong *R* in his name." She was happy.

"Was there anything else you want to tell me? I feel like there's more you are not telling me," she said.

"No. No. That's all. If you ever need me, please do not hesitate to call." I didn't want to spoil her birthday, but I had already noticed her brandings. A small, brown scar shaped like an oval with a squiggly line through it. *That's a voodoo marking*, I told myself.

"I need to come see you because I feel like there's more you need to tell me and you're not," Clotaire said.

A month later she made an appointment, which she quickly called and canceled later the same day. Three months later, she made another appointment on the phone with me, which she again canceled the next day. One day, Romy told me "the lady from the Millennium called and is coming by to see you right now."

Just then, she peeled into my driveway in her BMW screaming, "Your prediction came true!" out the window. She blurted the words as she got out, car still running. She hadn't even parked it. She looked elegant, but hardly composed. She pulled out a picture and said, "Here's the man you told me about."

In the photo, I saw the fair-complexioned man with big blue eyes, dancing the tango with her. She said his name was Rodrigo, and she had met him in Barcelona. They were both obsessed with tango. They were inseparable for three weeks, she said. When the time came for her to return, they made plans to buy property in Spain and live together. All she had to do was move.

"I want him! I love him!" she said.

"I know he cares about you," I said, "but you're going to have to fight for him. I see something blocking you from being in love and being happy with love."

"No matter what I do, I can't find happiness. I know he's my soul mate!" she said.

"Yes, I do feel there's a soul mate connection," I said. It really looked like true love in my visions.

"Look, I need your help. I'm Haitian. My real name is Clotaire Perrin. I come from a family of drug traffickers and voodoo priests, including my own mother. I, myself, was supposed to be sacrificed," she said as tears streamed down her face. My eyes popped out of my head. All the years of shame and fear went from her straight through me. I started to cry from all the heavy energy she laid on me. She told me everything she knew. Clotaire's story began in Port-au-Prince, about sixty years ago. Clotaire was designated to be the sacrificial lamb for voodoo priests before she was even born. Her mother, Mameio, a voodoo priestess, had fallen in love with a handsome, rich, white lawyer. But she was his servant, and she knew what that meant. The class distinction didn't apply in bed, apparently, because Mameio ended up getting pregnant with his seed and produced Clotaire.

All through the pregnancy, Mameio was convinced that the baby would be white, and the lawyer would then leave his wife for her. But just in case things didn't go as planned, she used voodoo to break up the man's marriage. She employed the use of a well-known voodoo priest by the name of Azzaca. Azzaca promised that, upon the announcement of her pregnancy, the marriage would be irretrievably broken. In return, he demanded the child upon birth for his ritual sacrifice. He said he would conceal this from the lawyer so that Mameio could say the child died suddenly, without warning.

Well, the lawyer left his wife after Mameio told him she was carrying their love child. But he told her in no way or at no time would he marry a Haitian servant. Really grinding that salt into the wound, he told her he never wanted to see her again. Mameio went crazy. She was grief-stricken. She never imagined her lover would not want her if he weren't married.

After the baby was born, the ritual began. Clotaire's grandmother, an unusually tall, massive, Christian woman, heard the ruckus, ran outside to a nearby field where her depraved daughter usually did her sorcery, and found Clotaire naked, on a tree stump in the dark, screaming while the group burnt her body with cigars. They were branding the baby, by a bonfire, ready to plunge a knife through the infant's heart.

Clotaire's grandmother, horrified and enraged, fought her way to the baby and slapped Mameio, telling her to go to the devil. Mameio fell on the fire in the scuffle and burned to death. The grandmother ran away with Clotaire. But Clotaire suffered bizarre brandings on her hands, on her neck, on the back of her legs, all over her body. She still has them today.

Her grandmother raised her with as much love as she could, but saw that Clotaire was easily led into hyper-fits during which she would scream that her mother was trying to kill her, that her mother was in her, hurting her and mocking her. Her grandmother decided the reason why Clotaire was tormented was because her mother's spirit was not resting. Instead it chose to haunt Clotaire.

When Clotaire turned nine years old, her grandmother died. She was left on her own, and she fell into the hands of her uncle, who used to beat her because he said he could see the devil in her. He would perform rituals that involved having her drink her own urine for purification and forced her to do penitential groundswork in a local church like a slave. By fifteen, she had turned to drugs and run off with a crack addict. She would mug people, steal, and break into homes. She was always stoned out of her mind. Then she got pregnant, and everything changed.

She thought of her own childhood, before her grandmother died, and she did not want to raise a baby in that manner. So she came to Miami to start over. One day, nine months pregnant, Clotaire looked through the classifieds, to see what kind of work she could do with her limited education, and there was an ad for a secretary for a law firm in Coral Gables.

Dan Bonner, a handsome, rich white real estate attorney, from the "old guard" in Miami, gave her the job. By the time her son was a year old, Dan had proposed. She couldn't believe her luck! He just fell for her. He was a multimillionaire. He adopted her son, supported her, and gave all the luxury life could offer.

But, after ten years of marriage, Bonner started cheating on her. When she found out, he told her it was because she could never have an orgasm. He said that because of this he never felt like a man. She moved out and into the Millennium downtown and went to real estate school. Soon she started selling major properties downtown through contacts she had cultivated over the years with Bonner. As soon as she could, she told Bonner she didn't want any of his money; she just wanted the divorce. He gave it to her, with a big, fat alimony check each month, with a clause that stated the alimony would cease if she cohabitated with anyone.

After many trials, she thought her life was back on track. The vacation to Spain had revitalized her. Meanwhile, she said while she tangoed in Spain, her friend Suzanne had found out about Clotaire's family's drug and voodoo past, both in Haiti and in Miami. She also discovered information about Clotaire's husband's infidelities and went to work discrediting Clotaire in her professional circles.

Then she set about turning Clotaire's downtown friends against her.

At the time there was also a rash of small break-ins in the luxury condos that were listed with the realty office. Many of them were Clotaire's listings. Of course, she was being accused of setting up the robberies. People who had known Clotaire for years now wanted no part of her. Realtors in her office would snub her, clutch their pocketbooks around her, and steal her clients. Finally, she was afraid that if her ex-husband, (who was paying her twenty thousand dollars a month alimony) ever found out about Rodrigo, he would cut her off.

"Please tell me, Regina . . . *can I have this man?*"

"Yes, but it's going to take work. You know you need help with your sexuality."

"I'm dead from the waist down," she said. *"I have no feeling in my vagina, Regina!!* I'll do anything! Nothing in the world means more to me than him!"

When you're a victim of voodoo and you're a woman, you always feel it in your uterus, ovaries, or vagina. All of that gets affected. Orgasms are the first to go. I told her I would need to consult my guides and sent her home.

Later I went into meditation. I saw *loas*, Haitian gatekeepers of the spiritual realm, all around her, eating a banquet around a large wooden table—*using her body as a plate.* I envisioned a tiny, wiry little man having sex with her while she slept. I wrote her mother's name on a piece of brown paper and stared at it.

"M-A-M-E-I-O."

Very few people realize the power of names. Most names are given by God, without a doubt, prior to a baby being born. This one was a particularly powerful name. I felt strong vibrations around the first three letters and knew this woman, who I saw as being statuesque and slim, was envious that her life had been cut off so quickly because of Clotaire and that love had always eluded her.

My guides revealed the truth about her mother to me. Mameio basically sold her soul to evil when she was just a teen, in a constant pursuit to seduce rich, white men. She had tried to kill Clotaire many times from beyond the grave—always on the night before her birthday because she had promised to kill her at birth. I knew Mameio was not gone. She was always around her, always watching. The bad karma that resulted from years of generational evil-doing haunted Clotaire. The truth is, undeservedly, you *will atone* for the sins of your forefathers.

I immediately drove to her condo downtown at high speed. My biggest dilemma was how to break some of the more graphic insights I had received about Mameio to the sophisticated and delicate Clotaire. I checked in with the bellman and took the elevator up, still packaging my presentation in the best possible manner. But when I reached Clotaire, she was already weeping hysterically. Rodrigo had left her, she said, because all the while they had been making love in Spain, she couldn't have an orgasm. She didn't make him feel like a man.

"Clotaire, there's more than orgasms affecting your life right now," I began. "Sit down. What I have to tell you is shocking and horrifying, but I have to come out and say it. As you know your mother tried to sacrifice you as a baby. She failed, but your mother's soul is trapped forever trying to fulfill her end of the bargain, which is, to kill you. Every night, the demons that were denied your life's blood have sex with you. On the eve of every birthday, when you think the bed's spinning and you hear pigs squealing, that's when they take you, Clotaire. When you wake up in the middle of the night, which I know you do because I've seen it, and you feel you can't breathe, as if someone was trying to suffocate you with a pillow, it's Mameio! How do you pretend not to know this?"

"Well . . . yes, I know it. I've gone looking for therapy, but . . . , well, it never worked! One psychologist forbid me to bring up anything like voodoo or my dead mother until we had gotten to 'what was really bothering me,' and another said she felt I was having 'anxiety attacks' because my husband was cheating on me. *Well of course it caused stress and anxiety!!* But not pigs squealing and beds spinning! Please Regina, you have to help me! I have to get better!!"

"And Clotaire, you must admit. You have an immense self-hatred for not being white. I've seen it. You scrubbed your own skin raw in the bath when you were a little girl because you thought you were supposed to be white. Mameio told you to do this as a little girl, didn't she? Your grandmother tried to keep you from doing this. But Mameio could reach your thoughts."

I confirmed all this with her, and I told her I had never dealt with so much black magic in my life.

"I really don't know what I can do for you because voodoo is not my specialty. You need to go to a voodoienne to clear it all out. The best is Erzulie, and she works out of a shop in Hialeah. You should go to her. I am just a psychic. I don't cast black magic spells. I work through the light."

"Please take whatever I have! I don't care if I have to live under a bridge. Money means nothing to me if I can't have happiness. I don't want to go to a strange voodoienne by myself! *Don't* make me go into this alone!!"

"Let me pray on it," I said.

My guides showed me that if I wanted to help, I could, but it wouldn't be easy. It would take all the energy I had. So I got rid of all my other clients. Clotaire kept me on retainer, for six hundred thousand dollars. The day we finally went to visit Erzvlie, gridlock through Hialeah during rush hour allowed for a strained prep course on Erzulie and what kind of work might be required to put Mameio's immortal soul to rest. My instincts told me "God is not taking Mameio," but, one never knew . . . Mameio had spent almost a lifetime doing evil, but she never killed Clotaire, or anyone we knew of, for that matter.

"Come in ladies. Regina, good to see you again. 'Ow ave you been? Business is slow this year, heh heh heh. How bout we get togetha and put a love spell on Miami and give evewywon a tewible case of adultery? Spwing is jus awound the corner, and I 'ave bills to pay. You know?" she cackled.

"Always a pleasure, Erzulie. We may indeed have to put a hex on all of Miami. But first, we need to rid her of her mother's evil spirit."

"And what as she done to you? I am an evil mother as well. My children had better not try to get rid of me!" again, cackling ferociously. Tiny bursts of spittle landed on my arm.

"This is Clotaire, Erzulie. She is from Haiti. Her mother was Mameio Ferrin, who worked under Azzaca."

"Well, Madame Clotaire. Are you a Vodoun princess or a lamb?"

"I am a lamb."

"Ooooh, no won is going to be abel to 'elp you, my dear. No won. Once a lamb, always a lamb, and it won't end until you die, *vous comprende pas?*" she said, mocking Clotaire. Sticking her tongue out and crossing her eyes.

"No! Please don't say that, Miss Erzulie! Regina told me you knew about my mother and about Azzaca. Please help us. I can't bear to live like this anymore!"

"'Ere ends the parable, for you do not choose what is your inheritance. But don't see in this a sign that all is written in Vodoun! No excuses, your Nanm (bad mojo) is yours to own. You have free will."

"Are you saying I have a choice? What choice? How is this a choice?! All my life I have been plagued by misery and pain!" Clotaire said, crying and sobbing.

Erzulie said nothing. She crossed her eyes again, baring her teeth.

"And if I believe I am the victim of Mameio—of Vodoun?" Clotaire said.

Erzulie stopped giggling.

"A vèvé is impermanent. It is the access code for the specific spiwit. Spread-legged you can dwaw it. With you feet you can erase it." *Vèvé* is a channel for spiritual invasion.

"How can I erase it with my feet?" Clotaire said.

I interrupted so Clotaire, who had been living solely in the white Miami world for more than she should have, could remember how they speak in voodoo—almost in riddles and song.

"She's saying walk back to the past, Clotaire. Walk backward to the place you were born," I said.

"I . . . I don't understand . . . I can't understand it . . . how can I walk back to . . . this . . . ?"

"Thank you once again for your time, Erzulie. Is there something we can take to help us?"

"Take a walk. *Loas* are not better or worse than we are," Erzulie said.

No words were spoken on the way home. Clotaire sat wild-eyed and tight-lipped. When we got back to my office, I told her what we were going to do.

"I'm going to do a binding on your Mameio. It will keep her from coming into my meditation and filling me with fear. I'll take a picture of a person and use white ribbon, sage, sulfur, mercury, and petrified wood. I bind ribbon around the picture. I say 'I'm binding you and all of your evil. You will not harm Clotaire; she is a child of God.' Then I burn the whole thing because when you do that, the fire, mixed with sage and sulfur, makes so much light that the darkness cannot enter. That's why when I pray on people, I leave candles burning constantly on their images. I will go to my chancel—a prayer room I rent inside a church in Boca Raton.

"Evil can't live in your heart, Clotaire. It can't live in your soul. It can only live in your mind. Make no mistake, evil exists. It plays with your mind. If the mind is not strong, the heart is not strong, and the heart and soul together are not strong. If you're weak, it defeats you. Do not give the devil a foothold. When fear and evil take over, your body starts to get sick. We're going to Haiti, Clotaire. We're going back to your tree stump."

She ran to the bathroom to vomit. After a few minutes, she came back and said, "Regina, I am desperate to rid myself of this *shit*. This sexual dysfunction, this fear! And the *hauntings* have made me a nervous wreck! But I'll be damned alongside *mon mere* before I wholly succumb. I'll buy our tickets, and we'll leave next week. I just need to tie up a few loose ends with Rodrigo."

I drove to Erzulie's that night to prepare. The witch charged me five thousand for the consultation.

"I need to know what to take and how to begin the undoing of the possession—the exorcism," I said.

"Take monay! Lots and lots of monay!" she cackled.

"How much?"

"Madame, anywon cannot do it. You must have passed *kanzo* indoctwination. Be a pwiestess. In all my yeeehs of expewience, I 'ave never known one to do it, wizzout elp fwom a pwiest or pwiestess. Dis is not a movie. You 'ave to seek Azzaca; 'e will be dere. 'E is not dead; he cannot die, dat I know for certain. And 'e is not stewpid. And 'e is not cheap. Go wit the understanding dat dis man 'as bank accounts in Kayman, in Bwazil, and in Euwope. What you seek requires significant animal sacwifice, cons'quently it is a vewy expensive service. Dis man 'as an army of *serviteurs*. 'E is a gweat artiste. 'E is the Voodoo King."

"And where I am gonna find him?" I asked.

"Croix-des-Missions," she answered without pausing.

The plane took off roughly. I kept sipping my soda, staring blankly ahead, thinking. Croix-des-Missions, Erzulie had told me, was a place known for illegal voodoo rituals for more than three hundred years. It used to be far enough on the outskirts of Port-au-Prince that the orgies could take place back "in the jungle," far away from prying *gendarmes'* eyes. It had also been the blood-drenched site of mass slaughters by slave owners and dictators alike. Now, it was a peaceful suburb, with a voodoo compound, a four hundred-year-old voodoo temple, and the country's Voodoo King ruling as its artist-in-residence.

Clotaire sat wild-eyed and frozen in her plane seat. I got up to go to the bathroom. I caught sight of my own face in the bathroom mirror: I, too, was wild-eyed and frozen. I hunched inside that incommodious little bathroom stall and cried like a baby.

"Oh Lord!" I cried out, "You are the One True God, through whom all good things come, though many have forsaken you! Your true flock invokes you, universally, as the patron of things despaired of. Pray for us who are so miserable. Pray that finally we may receive the comfort, consolation, and relief from all anxiety and your eternal peace."

We hardly spoke as we disembarked and found our chauffeur. He leaned against a rusty old Mercedes with torn leather seats. Driving was an obstacle course, avoiding sluggish, overloaded carts, and, by contrast, the "tap-taps," buses so crammed with men, women, babies, goats, chickens, and luggage, they flared out like fans while cutting hairpin turns. Huge metal trucks barreled through without slowing or stopping, with bicyclers weaving in and out of the lot like colorful ribbons. I rolled down the window and took a deep breath: smoke, burning wood, manure, urine, decay, fried food, and spirits—millions and millions of spirits. Then, bang! I got knocked off my seat by an enormous third-world pothole.

"Yo Dale!"

"Are you all right?" Clotaire asked me.

"Oh my God!" I said, laughing hysterically, rubbing my bruised butt.

"Worse than Spain!" Clotaire said, giggling maniacally.

So broke the dreadful silence on our two-hour journey from the airport through Port-au-Prince, to Croix-des-Missions, to find the Voodoo King. His little compound soon came into sight. Azzaca's voodoo paintings lined the entrance of a thatched-roof temple, nestled within a compound of buildings. They were enormous depictions of smiling brown Virgin Marys wielding machetes; green men bleeding orange liquid from their ribs into a cup; and tiny twin black cherubs dancing on the back of a naked white woman, asleep on the ground. I finally started to get the picture, so to speak, of why this man was the "Voodoo King." The chauffeur stopped short.

"What's the matter? Is he stuck?" I asked Clotaire.

"He said he won't go any further. We'll have to walk."

A big-hipped woman in a spotless white dress met us on a footpath. She said something in Creole to which Clotaire replied and handed her the envelope with the cash. Clotaire never told me how much she paid. Clients have a tendency to lean cheap. I prayed Clotaire had been generous. Grimy and half-possessed myself, I mopped my brow with a piece of airplane toilet paper I'd kept in my pocket. We followed Big Hips into the temple. Inside the small white room were the same type of copper bowls Erzulie had back in her voodoo shop filled with "monay." A tiny man, with a wide, flat nose, and big, broad smile sat cross-legged in the floor, sketching on a canvass. It was Azzaca.

The rumor was he'd been born sometime before 1900, but there wasn't a gray hair on his head. He was completely devoid of any wrinkles.

I suspected he'd sooner slit our throats than help us, but we breathed a unanimous sigh of relief, anyway. He said something in Creole to Clotaire, who stood frozen by the door. Again, he repeated something I didn't understand, like a question.

"Answer him! We didn't come all this way for nothing!" I said.

She answered him, and he went back to painting. I dropped the bit of toilet paper on the floor, marched over to Clotaire, turned her 'round, lifted her blouse and screamed, *"Look at this mark. It's one of your voodoo marks. Give her her life back!!"*

She went berserk, screaming, "No! I can't do this, Regina! I don't want to do this! It reminds me of my mother! It reminds me of my mother!"

I said, "Stop it! Stop it, right now! This is what we came for! Now do what he says!"

Across the middle of her back was a thick serpent-shaped scar. Azzaca got up and poked it with his finger, and it opened up. Clotaire was crying hysterically. Smoke wheezed out of the raw, scarlet slit. Clotaire spoke to Azzaca. I think she was telling him what she knew about her story. His eyes never left the marks. My guides told me not to be scared. We were protected, and Azzaca knew it. Whatever we wanted, no matter how far-fetched, would soon come to pass.

Then he said, in English, "Where's the rest?" She turned, holding the blouse in front of her breasts, shaking her head and screaming, "Regina, please help me! Help me! For God's sake, help me!!"

Azzaca's voice thundered through the tiny temple, "Show me! Show me!"

"No! God No!"

"Show me! Show me at once!" he said grabbing her by the elbow and leading her outside. I ran along the footpath trying my best to be brave for Clotaire.

He led her to a huge, stumplike table, surrounded by a white chalk line. Four white candles in four corners were melted on the top. Four bowls were carved into the corners. Two leather straps hung off the sides, stained with blood. I assumed it was Clotaire's stump. Clotaire was crying hysterically now, and I admit my feet said, "Run," but my guides said, "*Stay.*"

He told her to lie back on the table and spread her legs. There on her inner thighs next to her vagina were the rest of the marks. From his pocket, he pulled out a razor-sharp penknife and stuck it into the side of the stump. No Gypsy would ever believe this. He asked her to call out the name of her mother and of lovers past and present.

"I can't! I can't! I can't do this. I'm dead inside! I can't feel it!! No man will ever want me like this! I'm dead!"

I held her arms down and said, "Clotaire, you've only been here for three minutes. This has been a part of your life for sixty years! Since you were born! I'm doing my best! Listen to him! We have no other way!"

But Clotaire was acting as if she was possessed by a demon—foaming and cursing. Then she went into convulsions. Azzaca didn't flinch. Her body was jerking uncontrollably while he chanted all these things in Creole I couldn't understand. He seemed to be calling all the demons out of her. Her head whipped back and forth. He held her down by her forehead and plunged the knife deep into her heart. At that moment the sun turned blood red. I knew that there was something upon us. Her body was writhing like a snake. A thunderbolt cracked so loudly it shook the sky as he lifted the knife out of her heart. Then he wiped it on his shirt and slid it back in his pocket.

Clotaire was still crying, but not bleeding. Did Azzaca perform a *bujo*, a Gypsy trick? I hugged Clotaire, sweating on her like a pig. A few people came over to us and helped Clotaire off the stump.

"Go. Go now and never return to Haiti!" he said. "Your life is of no use to us now."

Azzaca spoke something in Creole to the big-hipped lady in white, and she escorted us back to our chauffeur. Our chauffeur, who wouldn't drive us up to the compound, but had made us walk the footpath, was cowering in the driver's seat. Clotaire slept on the ride back to Port-au-Prince. That night, in my hotel bed, I had a nightmare. I dreamt the big-hipped woman in white came to me and started tugging at the hem of my nightgown, whispering, "Give yourself to me tonight. Submit to my will, and I'll give you anything you want."

She grabbed my ankle and held me down while also grabbing at my breasts and slipped her hands under my nightie, caressing my thigh, while I struggled to get free.

"No! No! Stop it! God please stop it!" I cried in my dream.

The struggle seemed endless, and suddenly I awoke, on the floor, with my gown pulled up over my head. For hours I tried to recall how such a thing could have happened, and then I remembered a story I heard once in my psychic circles. A white lady in her mid-thirties once went to get some supplies from a voodoo store. She bought two candles and a stick of palm butter. She paid with a check and threw a piece of gum she'd been chewing into the trash can. That night she dreamt she was raped by seven or eight demons.

The story goes that the gum that had been in her mouth carried her essence, her saliva, and the voodoienne was able to possess her through it. Sweat, urine, and feces all carry a person's essence, but saliva, the liquid that comes directly from the place where words can be spoken, is the strongest because of the power of words. I had mopped the sweat off my brow with a piece of toilet paper and left it at the voodoo temple. It just goes to show you how even an experienced psychic can become the prey of the Voodoo King. It was definitely him, in the guise of the big-hipped woman—just to mess with me. I swear they're the devil's pranksters.

But it gave me an idea. As soon as we got back from Haiti, I put Clotaire on a sex regimen.

"We have to revive your femininity," I said. "We will start very small—tiny, even—with a thong."

I told Clotaire to buy the sexiest, raunchiest lingerie she could find and take time out every day for thirty minutes to wear it and fantasize about Rodrigo. To really want him and think about his body, his voice, and his smell, until it put her in a trance-like state. I told her to really think about his hands over her, pleasing her, teasing her, and making her want more. I gave her goat's milk baths with white roses and a mixture of herbs to make her feel more feminine.

"I feel better. I'm starting to visualize myself with Rodrigo better. I don't feel the shame or that sex is dirty. I don't think I do. I want to go back to see Rodrigo."

That month there was a tango festival in Madrid. Her aura got lighter and lighter. She looked refreshed. She bought new clothes and a beautiful new tango outfit. Before she left I reminded her, "If he truly loves you, he won't acknowledge your past actions or reactions. And remember now to walk forward. Keep walking forward."

"Thank you, Regina. I don't know what just happened to me, but I feel . . . well . . . My God, I feel . . . cured . . . I think. I don't know how to repay you. I really must have looked like a crazy lady when I came to you! Did you really, really see my mother? Did you see all the evil that she did to me? How she tried to have me killed so many times?"

"Yes, I did see her," I reassured her, "but I don't see her in your future."

Clotaire was cured, and there was eventual success with Rodrigo.

FIFTEEN

Can't Buy Me Love

've been told that Gypsy women have been described in history as "astoundingly beautiful" by a preacher who traveled through Pennsylvania back in the 1700s. He spent a great deal of time writing about them, in his accounts of "The Black Dutch," who were not really black and not really Dutch. They were Gypsies: horse-traders and basket-makers. They settled in the area near the Amish and Mennonite communities because they had Germanic roots. This really means they were kicked out of Germany or fled because some lord wanted their heads as trophies for his mantel.

Well, whether "The Black Dutch" women really were "astoundingly beautiful" is anybody's guess, but here, in South Florida, Gypsy princesses are *hot*. And, as I said before, they're not allowed to date or be touched by any *gaje* (non-Gyp).

One summer, I took off for the Bahamas for a week and came back tan and sexy. I bleached my hair blonde for a change, from my usual dark brown. Soon after, I appeared on a local TV talk show on psychics. A few days after the show, I got a phone message.

"This is Mack Kent. I live in Palm Beach, and I saw you on TV. I must say, you are extraordinarily beautiful. I am in need of your psychic services. Please call me."

When I called him back, he asked how much the reading was. At the time, my readings were five hundred dollars an hour, and I told him where my office was. Then he said, "Oh no. No, I can't come down. I'll give you my address." His voice was shaky but controlled.

"Well, I'll have to charge you extra because I don't usually make house calls."

"All right. Are you any good?"

"You'll just have to find out," I said, hating that question more and more each day.

When I arrived, I saw a mansion worth about twenty-five million. It was in the *real* Palm Beach, the older section on the *actual* beach (not Palm Beach *County* where the wanna-bes live). These are beachfront "cottages" for those of dizzying wealth and questionable mores. A long driveway set back from the road led to the house. It was lined with beautiful sable palms. Practically every bit of the rectangular house was tinted glass so you couldn't see inside. I rang the doorbell.

He said, "I looked through the peephole and watched for you," as he opened the door. "If you looked dangerous, I wouldn't have let you in."

His eyes never left me. He said, "You really keep yourself up! That's a smart skirt you're wearing. It suits you, your shape, I mean. Is that a Cartier ring?"

"Thanks. Yes."

"I've been to a lot of psychics, and I can tell you really do well."

While we walked through the house to the kitchen, he told me little about himself. He told me he was seventy-three years old and used to play professional baseball, which I believed because he was very tall and still pretty muscular. He had salt-and-pepper hair and a youthful demeanor. My overall impression was that of a very clean-cut man who looked and acted much younger than his years. Everything in his house was chic and tasteful.

"I like the way you've decorated," I complimented him.

"My ex-wife decorated," he replied.

After that he kept wanting to talk about my marriage, how long I'd been married, how many kids I had, and what my husband did.

I said, "Mr. Kent, I hate to rush you, but I came up here to do a reading for you, and I only have a certain amount of time before rush hour. I'm sure you know what it is like to drive to Miami on I-95 in rush hour."

"Yes, sorry. Okay, well let's do it then," he said.

The divorce came up immediately. I saw the wife wanted a lot more than half.

"Tell me," he started, "is she going to take me down? Am I going to have to file for bankruptcy?"

But the cards showed he had more homes and investments of which his wife was unaware. I said, "No, you won't. You'll be fine."

He said, "Look again! Look again!" while he kept touching my hands. It was clear it was sexual. I did not respond kindly. I pulled my hands away and said, "Let's continue the reading, okay?"

I continued, "I see your wife is a good woman. But she suffered some emotional abuse from you, and she stopped sleeping with you."

"That woman had everything she could ever want. I gave her everything I had! I couldn't have been any more generous and nice! She abused *me*! Nothing was ever good enough. You got one thing right; she stopped sleeping with me!"

"Look, Mr. Kent, I can only tell you what I see in the reading. And I do see that she was abused emotionally by you. She is passive-aggressive, so she stopped sleeping with you. And that hurt you deeply," I said.

He squeezed my knee. One part of me said *"Shit!"* The other part of me said, "He's like a grandfather; maybe he's just squeezing like a grandfather?"

I said, "Mr. Kent, you have been very callous and very hard on your people, your kids included. And you haven't given women much respect or attention."

"What's wrong with me?" he asked.

"Well, first of all, you have a fear of being alone, and you are getting exactly what you fear," I told him.

"I don't want to be alone. You're right. I never wanted to be alone," he kept repeating.

171

I told him I'd mail him some candles to burn and that I would send some prayers for him to recite so he could cleanse himself. This case was not a hard case. Late in life, many people have a change of heart. When the glamour is gone, the children are grown, and there's nothing left to prove, they look around and think about what is really important. They consider changes they can make to improve the short time they have left. They take the choice that's least hypocritical.

Then he asked, "I'm going on a date this weekend. What do you think—is she right for me?"

"I see her chemistry is wrong for you, actually," I said. "But I do see you will be great friends."

"You're right. But I don't want to be alone again. Not tonight. What are you doing tonight?"

I said, "I'm going home to be with my kids."

"Can't blame a guy for trying!" he chuckled. I smiled, but raised my eyebrow, giving him that, "Oh, I can't, *can't I?*" look. I continued the reading and reassured him again that I saw he would actually lose a lot less than he anticipated. He gave out a whoop and kissed me on the cheek—way, way too close to my lips.

I said, "Okay. Well, I can see you're very happy about this! But try to contain yourself!"

"Oh Regina, I know I just met you but I wish I could find a girl like you! I wish I could meet someone like you! I wish I'd met you a long time ago."

"Maybe you can; let's look into it," and I continued to read.

He said, "Hey, before we begin that, I want to show you my swimming pool."

"But I'm kind of in the middle of . . ."

"Please? I think you've never seen this kind of pool. This was custom-made. Let me show you?"

"Okay, Mr. Kent, but only for a minute," I said, reluctantly.

He was right, though. It was *magnificent*. It had two plunging waterfalls with ledges, so you could stand behind the water and let it close in around you like a curtain, and several pod-shaped Jacuzzis at each end.

There was a round swim-up bar in the middle with a bridge next to it for the staff. It looked like it belonged at a resort.

He said, "Bring the kids sometime! They'd love it!"

I said, "Thank you, but I have a pool. Granted, not as nice as yours, but I have one. We do okay."

He led me outside to walk around the lanai.

"Let me tell you a funny story," he said. "Let me tell you what I did one night. I went out with this woman. We went out for coffee. We both started talking about our divorces, and she burst out crying, saying, 'Gee Mack, I don't know what I'm gonna do! I don't think I'll have any money after this divorce!'

"I said to her, 'Cheer up! You can always be a hooker!' And she says, 'Mack, I have grown children! I have a respectable life! I could never be a hooker!' And she never spoke to me again! Do you think that was insulting, Regina?"

"Yes, Mr. Kent, I do," I said, now wishing I hadn't heard it.

"Women don't get me," he said, looking down at his feet.

Of course Mack never saw her again. Even I thought this was a heartless joke. Who would ever trust him when he took a serious moment and made it an opportunity to show the woman how worthless her life really was to him. He was very insensitive to women. But what bothered me most was that he *really didn't* feel bad about it. He was using it to test me.

"I wish I could just meet a nice girl like you and settle down, Regina. You look Italian. God, you're beautiful," he said. "Have I told you today how gorgeous you are?"

I laughed. "You have—three times. And you will again, I'm sure. Let's go back and finish the reading."

We sat down, and I opened up another card and saw that he was mean to his children and that all of his ex-wives were on antidepressants. The children were in limbo, without affection from their father or their mothers.

I said, "Mr. Kent, you need to do something about your children. They are neglected and sad. This will come back to haunt you. You must

173

ask forgiveness from them. And you must try to see them more often. My spirit guides tell me this is what is making you feel bitter and utterly alone."

"They're not children anymore. They're grown men and women. Anyway, they hate me. All they want is my money."

"It may seem so, Mr. Kent, but they're children who have never learned to communicate their feelings. You must open up that door." Then I prayed with him for love between him and his children. He asked me to show him how to pray. I told him, "The Bible says you just need to talk to God, tell him what is in your heart."

I felt like his heart was trying sincerity on for size because I could feel him focus on the kids.

"Look, Mr. Kent, umm, Mack, you can change all this. You will do well in the divorce. You will have money and time to do wonderful things with your life. Spend that time with your kids, and do right by them, and love will follow. That's just my opinion. That's it, Mr. Kent. You can make of life what you want. It is yours."

He handed me a fat stack of hundreds.

"I'm going to Connecticut for court in a week. Will you read me again when I get back?"

"If you think it's necessary," I said.

"Yes. Yes I do. I want to focus on the children this time."

I said "Okay" and made my way to the door. Then he gave me more money—a huge tip.

When he returned, he called and asked me to come over again for another reading. I thought about what he said about wanting to focus on his kids, and for them, I went. But I took my husband, Romy, with me so he could wait for me in the car. I just had this feeling.

He had a present waiting for me when I walked in.

"You did it! You were right on the money, Regina!!" he said, pouring. "You're right. I won't have to pay her a cent of my investments, and I'm keeping this house and the one in Santa Barbara! I have something for you!"

I said, "Mr. Kent, you don't need to buy me anything."

"No, no I didn't buy it! I got it from the house in Connecticut. It's a painting. Here, take it," he said, handing it to me. It looked like a Manet, but I wasn't sure. At any rate, I loved it. But I felt it was too much.

"This is beautiful, Mr. Kent, but I can't accept this."

"Please! Please take it. I want you to have it. I insist."

"Fine, I can see your mind is made up. I guess there's nothing left to say other than thank you," I said.

I gave him a reading about his relationship with his kids and left. He squeezed my knee again, but he saw my husband waiting for me in the car. I felt him let go of any sexual urges toward me.

I brought the painting home, figuring I would give it to someone eventually. But from the moment I got home, he kept calling and calling and calling with feedback about his kids. "They don't love me," he'd say, or "They won't talk to me."

I kept telling him to keep trying; it would happen. "Show them your goodness," I said, "and things will fall into place."

"No! No! No, I can't keep trying. You've got to help them open up! Please do something!" he insisted.

"Okay, look, Mr. Kent—Mack. I'll do a kindness spell on them, to make them more receptive to you. Do you have any personal articles that belong to them?"

"Yes I do! Come over, Regina! I have plenty of things!"

"Mail them to my office," I said.

"Oh no, I can't. Too many to pick from. I want you to select the best things for the spell," he said.

"Fine." I finally gave up. "I'll come over tomorrow."

"I'm leaving town tomorrow. Come over tonight."

"Alright."

He didn't lie. He had pictures and letters and affidavits with their signatures, and clothing that belonged to his kids all over the house. It was easy to pick something small for the work I had to do. Then he handed me a box.

"What's this?" I asked, warily.

"For you, my beautiful witch."

"Mack, I'm not a witch."

"I know, I know, just open it!"

Inside the box were a Hermes scarf, a Chanel belt, and an envelope with five thousand dollars.

"I can't accept this, Mack."

"Please, you help me so much. You help the kids. Please take it. For all the phone calls."

Weeks went by with a few calls from Mack every day. *Maybe he really is just lonely*, I thought. So I called him one time, without prompting, just to check on him. Well, he was so happy! He invited me to have lunch with him at his house and do another reading about a woman he met at a singles party. So I went, and along came Romy, just in case.

I walked in and got a big greeting: hugs, kisses—huge sloppy wet ones on my cheeks close to my mouth. I stiffened. I walked to the kitchen table, and I got the cards out of my totebag.

"Wait, before we do that, I want to show you what I've done to the bedroom. You'll really appreciate this!" he said.

"Let's do the reading first," I said, because I got the feeling he was up to something.

"No, Regina, really, I did something you'd love to the bedroom. I was inspired."

"Okay. Why don't you show me real quick, and then we'll see what is going on with this woman you met at the party," I said. I thought, *What could he possibly try while Romy's out in the car? What would he be brazen enough to try?*

He stepped away to let me walk in first, and I didn't like that. Then he sat on the bed and said, "See? I changed the style in here to reflect the new me! I have some candles and some books on parenting and tarot cards! Come sit down on the bed with me, Regina. This is really a magnificent bed! My ex-wife bought this, but she can't get it back because I'm in love with it! Sit on it with me. I swear you'll love the way it feels."

"That's it, Mr. Kent! I'm not . . ."

I tried to protest but he pulled me toward him, trying to fondle me. Still in shock, I screamed, "What are you doing? The guides are watching! Shame on you!" But it did not discourage him. He continued to try to have his way with me. All I could think of while trying to free myself from his hold was *Dear God, how can this be happening to me?* His strength was that of a wild animal.

Somehow, by the grace of God, I was able to wrench free, and I ran out the bedroom door, leaving my pocketbook, wallet, tote bag, everything inside. I ran down the hall, out the front door, and started screaming for Romy out on the lawn.

"Start the car, Romy! Start the car!!"

Romy freaked out and jumped out of the car.

"What happened, Gina? Why are your clothes all messed up? What the hell did that bastard do?"

"Get in the car! Get in the car! Let's just get out of here! Just go! Go!"

Romy and I peeled out of the driveway, and I looked back in time to see Mack swinging my pocketbook by a finger in his doorway.

"That bastard! He's taunting me to come back! I don't fucking believe this motherfucker! What the hell do I do, Romy?"

"Leave it Gina! We can't do anything! Leave it to God!"

That night, I got about a hundred messages from Mack. Some threatening, some apologetic, others blaming *me* for what happened. The next day he accused me of seducing him to steal the painting and rob him of more than thirty thousand dollars. Four days later, I got a package in the mail with all my stuff and gifts from Cartier, and a note:

Dearest Regina,

Forgive me. It's just that I was captivated by your intense beauty. Please don't be angry with me. I need another reading. Call me.

MACK

SIXTEEN

Model Makeover

South Beach had become an international destination for the modeling and film industry. My office was constantly overrun by gorgeous models wanting beauty spells, love spells, and money spells. Romy was also constantly in and out of my office, doing the books, painting the prayer room, or putting up shelves.

One afternoon, I came back from the Louis Vuitton shop at Bal Harbor, happy as a clam with my new Suhali. I had also bought some new Chanel lipstick and lip liner from Saks and wanted to try it on. When I opened the door to the bathroom, lo and behold, there was Romy, in the arms of one of my clients, a gorgeous Brazilian model.

"Oh my God! Romy! You bastard! Get out! Get out!!"

I threw anything I could get my hands on at them—towels, baskets, soap. The girl ran out of the bathroom, grabbing a towel to cover herself as she flew by me, long brown hair flowing behind her. Romy, however, was cowering on the floor, begging me not to leave him.

"Gina-babe! G! Please forgive me! I'm crazy! *Dilo sim!* You're the eyes in my head! What did I do? I'm so ashamed! I'm only a man! You been working a lot, babe, and you . . . you haven't been . . ."

"*Don't!!* Don't you dare try to blame me, you piece-of-shit. Get out! I pay the bills, I pay the rent, I don't need you!

"No! G! I'm sorry! I'm crazy! I'm a bad person! Just don't leave me! I'll kill myself!"

"You don't do shit! Just sit around spending my money and eating. You're a big fat slob, Romy! Get out and don't come back to me!" I screamed, shoving his fat ass out the doorway and kicking him into the hallway. Some workers from the designer's studio poked their heads out, cocking their attitude glasses up and dropping their jaws.

"Get out you piece-of-shit!"

An embarrassment like getting thrown out of your own house by your wife is worse on a Gypsy man than getting caught by your wife with a Brazilian model. We call it *lashave*. You must never look bad to another Gypsy. If you have *lashave*, you won't get a "chair." That means you won't get invitations to the best and biggest affairs in town by the Gypsy elite. No will come to you for advice. And no one will mourn you when you die. *That* is the biggest insult.

Romy tried to change my mind repeatedly about kicking him out. He went to my father, but he said, "Romy, you fucked up. Now you gotta make up for it. Buy her a diamond. Take her on a trip. And don't do it again—at least don't let her catch you."

Then he went to my brothers. "You're a dumbass! How did you get caught? You know what, Romy? Spare us the details. Do what you gotta do and put your family back together!"

Then he appealed to my children. "You gotta speak for me. Talk to your mother. I'm your father. You can't live without me! Speak to her and beg her to let me come home!"

"Dad, whatever you did made Mom very sad and very tired. Dad you gotta fix it, or we're gonna be like the *gaje*! You're going to get a divorce!"

Can you believe it? My babies were growing up so fast. But I had no interest in talking to Romy. I had no interest in anything. I stopped going shopping, stopped psychic counseling, stopped taking care of the kids, and hired a full-time nanny. I stopped eating, bathing, and sleeping. Even though I'd dropped out of life, I worried so much about everything that I had stress. I was nervous all the time. Not even during the time I was counseling George did I feel so *off*.

I talked to my mother about what happened, to decide for myself whether or not I even wanted to be married anymore.

She said, "All things are simple. All things are the way they are. There is is no use in trying to make rules or ask why."

I thought about getting a reading for myself, but no self-respecting Gypsy would ever go for a psychic reading. It's an unwritten rule. We have our own, older gypsy women who are healers, and we'll take help from them as long as it's kept secret. But mostly we don't get readings because we don't want other Gypsies to know our weak spots. That's *lashave*. A Gyp can't bear looking weak to another Gypsy.

So, two weeks later I took the opportunity to try a little of the *gaje* magic. Because there are not supposed to be any drugs in the Gypsy culture, I went to a *gaje* shrink. To be honest, I was always looking to experience something new regardless of the circumstance. The doctor put me on an antidepressant and told me that in a few days I'd start to feel better. I did—but slowly. I discovered that I missed work, the kids, and shopping, but I didn't miss Romy. I couldn't leave Romy either. In Gypsy culture, when a man cheats, he gets everything and a pat on the back.

After six months, I finally ventured into the office, quietly, avoiding the design studio at all costs. I checked my messages. A stream of "Please call me, Regina. I'm dying!" came out of the answering machine. All were from models wondering if they "got the job." I started with the one that sounded the most insipid to get her out of the way.

"Hi. Um . . . my name is Christina. Um . . . I got your number through a friend. I heard you're, like, really good. I'm having some . . . uh . . . problems. Can you please call me back? I need a reading, like, soon, please. Thanks, and please call me soon, okay?" she said.

I called her back and asked her to stop by. Meanwhile, I had to go pee—in the *bathroom*. No one had been here since I had caught Romy. I'd forbidden anyone to return to the office, and it was filthy in there. I used it out of utter necessity because though I had originally thought I would rather walk one hundred fifty miles to a gas station than use this bathroom, when you gotta go, you gotta go. Maybe it was time to reclaim my own damn office bathroom!

"Hello . . . ?" I heard a lady's voice coming from the hall as I finished up.

"Hi," I said straightening up. A very tall, bony woman with a short platinum bob haircut swept in. She was striking, but a little gaunt.

"Hi. I'm Christina, the model who called you. Can you do a reading for me right now?" she asked.

I looked in her big, green, dumb eyes. She looked hopelessly self-absorbed.

"How old are you?" I said.

"Twenty-seven."

"How long you been a model?" I asked.

"Um, well, I've always been modeling for, like, a catalogue, or something. My mom started me in pageants when I was, like, three years old and stuff, so, you know . . ."

We walked back to my desk and sat down.

"Have you ever had any type of reading done before?" I asked.

"Well, yeah, like, this one time . . . this lady held my hand and told me stuff about me, but it was very general," she replied.

I said, "Okay. Then you know that some readings can be very general if you don't focus on one issue. Focus on what you want to know."

Her energy was virtually nonexistent. I shuffled the cards.

Then she said, "Well, I can't get a job. I can't get a man, I can't pay my bills, and I'm losing all my friends. Do you feel a bad vibe from me?"

She explained that for months she hadn't been able to get any legitimate modeling assignments. If she got one, she lost it at the booking because the clothes wouldn't fit her, or her hair was wrong, or something was amiss. So she went on a high-protein diet similar to the South Beach Diet to lose weight and now couldn't hold anything down, leaving her bowels terribly weak. Three months ago she'd been sent on a booking to New York, but it had been a fake. The supposed clients drugged and raped her.

She was also being sexually harassed by a club owner where she worked between modeling jobs and had to tiptoe around him when it was time for her to leave for the night. If he saw her leaving, he would make her stay longer and talk to him for hours about what he wanted to do with her sexually. I told her that I would do a quick meditation while she was near me.

"Okay, concentrate on your problem, while I focus on you. I see that three years ago, you were one of the best models on the beach. The best! You got paid hand over fist and never had a problem with men. You had one guy you lived with."

"Yes! Yes! Exactly! My boyfriend dumped me, and I haven't had a date since! I was always getting calls for bookings. My booking agent loved me! Oh, but now they hate me. They all hate me! No one wants me anymore!" Christina said.

"I see you went to the islands a lot, too. You went to Jamaica all the time."

"Yes, I have a great friend who runs Strawberry Hill, in Kingston. It's a hotel and spa, and I used to be invited, like, every weekend. You're freaking me out! Totally!"

"I see you're going to get a new car! Yes—and I see a lawsuit around you. The outcome will be favorable."

"Yeah! That's right. I'm suing someone else for sexual harassment."

"I see you will also get a new job. Very soon."

"Really? You're sure?"

"Absolutely."

"Oh my God! That's great! I'm so happy! Thank you! Thank you so much for the reading! I've heard you were very good, but you're incredible!"

When she left, I went back into the bathroom and cleaned up. I was back to normal; the shock was over. Thank God for antidepressants.

The weeks that followed were almost pleasant. I smiled a lot. I hired a new, part-time nanny, I cooked some Gypsy comfort food for the kids— a big skillet of *sadme*, rice, olives, and pork—sort of a spicy paella. I talked to Romy a few times on the phone.

For the time being, Romy was living with his brother who was keeping him out of the kindness of his heart. I'd changed the locks and hired an ex-Sandinista hitman to shoot him on sight if he came within three hundred yards of Hibiscus Island. But Romy could have had me tossed out of my own house if he'd wanted. In the Rom community, a husband can leave his wife for any reason, at any time. A wife may not leave her husband arbitrarily unless the *Baro* approves it based on frequent and extraordinarily violent physical abuse. Romy's family paid good money for me to my parents. It would shame and embarrass them if I left Romy.

Then there were the kids—two by this time. They would also be shamed if I got a *gaje* divorce. Romy and I would be overcharged like crazy when it came time for my sons to buy a wife. There was also the small problem of custody. In our culture, the man takes all.

I didn't hate Romy. I hated the stress we caused each other. And I was tired of having to support the family by myself.

So I popped the pills like Tic Tacs and conveniently forgot to address any of these issues. One afternoon, the phone rang as I was getting the mail.

"Regina, this is Christina. I got fired from the club last week, and I drank so much I crashed my Beemer. I totaled it. It's gone, and I have no money to get a new one. My mom says I can have her Ford Escort. It's, like, ten years old. And, guess what? I got another job at another club, right away and stuff, but it pays hardly anything."

"Hmm . . . I have no idea why this is happening, Christina. I am so sorry these things are happening. Let me meditate on this."

I ran into the prayer room in my house and closed the door. I sat down cross-legged and relaxed and let my spirit guides lead me. I started my breathing techniques, but my jeans were cutting into my abdomen so badly I couldn't breathe. I looked down and saw how thick my waist had become. I undid the top button on my jeans.

The messages I picked up were mixed, coming in several at a time.

They were vague, almost like when the TV cable goes out. Several screens appeared to me at once. I almost stopped trying until I saw a vision of Christina and what I thought was a new man. Then I saw her at her lawyer's office, and she was smiling. I called her at once.

"Christina?"

"Yes?"

"It's me, Regina. I just this minute went in to meditation for you, and I have to tell you that I saw you got a new boyfriend. It looks like you definitely came out ahead on the lawsuit."

"Oh my God! You're sure?"

"Yes. I promise."

"Oh my God! Awesome! Okay, Thanks!"

Three months later, I wasn't feeling well again. I was very tired and sad, so I made some homemade soup. The kids were outside playing with the nanny, and I was slicing carrots when the phone rang.

"Hello?"

"Regina, this is Christina. I'm sorry to have to ask you this, but I want my money back."

"Why? What happened?"

"You said you saw me winning this lawsuit, but it got thrown out, and now I'm being fined or sued or something, for a frivolous lawsuit, I think it's called."

"Oh my gosh!"

"Yeah, and that man you saw with me? It's the sexual harasser. He got me pregnant!"

"What? I didn't know you were having sex."

"Well, I had to. Sometimes he harasses me so much I have to sleep with him for him to stop. Now I'm for sure pregnant, and he's asking me to marry him, and I hate his fucking guts, Regina! I fucking hate him!"

"Well, you simply won't marry him, then. Let me meditate on this. Jesus, I have no idea why this is happening!"

I started to laugh, thinking about the irony. How my predictions were now completely the opposite of the outcomes creating a heinous situation for the simpleton.

"Are you laughing at me?" she asked.

"No, no, I've got a cough, I'm sorry. Anyway, look, I have to run now. I've got calls to make, so I'll meditate on this and call you back, okay?"

"Actually, I think I want my money back. I think you're full of shit, and you fucked up my life. So I think you need to give me back my thousand dollars for these bullshit readings and meditations. I'm so sure you're, like, not even a real psychic."

"Christina, I'm sorry you feel that way. This has never happened to me, in my entire career. But remember, I did see what had happened in the past. So I need to try to figure out what's happened to my visions of the future."

"Maybe so, but I need a refund!"

"Of course. Of course, you'll get it. Don't worry."

I went straight to the grocery store to buy white roses and vinegar so I could perform a ritual cleansing. I was convinced my energy was low because of my disdain for my job.

That night I drew a warm bath with white rose petals, holy water, and my signature perfume. Then I pasted photographs of my children and me on the walls. I slipped into the bath and meditated on clearing out all the negative energy that surrounded me, scattering it to the four corners and ridding myself of ill will, cynicism, and depression.

I had two visions. In the first, I stood on a small hill overlooking a university. Over the rolling hills flew a huge black cloud, and it got closer and closer. As it drifted over my head, I saw it was actually a fishing net full of bats. The bats were flying the net over my head and into a wooded area, directly behind me. The bats were struggling to get free, but the net held them tight.

In the second vision, I stood in a large field, under a full moon. A long, intricate spiderweb stretched across and over me from my left, all the way to a distant tree about a half mile away on my right. It was covered with the carcasses of little animals and bugs. Smack above my head sat its creator, an immense, brown, hairy spider. It sprang from the web and chased me all over the field trying to bite me. I was confused, but not terrified. I eluded the spider and the web.

The next day I went to see my shrink to get a refill for my prescription. "Thanks for seeing me, Doctor Skimmer," I said.

"Oh no problem, Regina. You're fine. I had you down for next week, but I understand you have some issues you want to discuss today?"

"I sure do. I had some problems with a client, and I feel like I'm losing my gift."

"And what gift is that? The psychic thing?"

"Yes. I'm predicting the opposite of what is going to happen, and I can't fix it. This has never happened to me before, and I'm gonna lose my mind if I can't get it back."

Dr. Skimmer never believed in my gift, never. I knew that, but I had nowhere else to go. If I went to the Gypsies, even the elders, I would get laughed out of town for *lashave*, for losing my gift. They'd love my misfortune. They'd relish it. I'd never live it down. So the best thing was to try to get some guidance from the *gaje*.

He said, "Gina, at some point, you're going to have to let that 'gift' go and try to focus on yourself. You know you have a great gift for counseling. You may want to try to earn your degree and become a therapist."

"Yes, I know. But what do you think about the opposite factor here?"

"I think you are trying to come out of your shell, a little bit, subconsciously. I think you're sick of the roller coaster and want real help. What do you think?"

"I think you're saying I need an education and a degree and to quit this psychic business."

"The stress would lighten up a bit. Maybe you shouldn't 'demand' that 'your gift' return, but concentrate instead on moving forward, without your 'gift.' Do you think you want to focus on what would help you move forward?"

I thought, *What a crock. This guy is useless.* I may never have gone to college, but even without psychic gifts, Gypsies know that an education obtained with money is sometimes worse than no education at all.

And then I saw my sign!

He had a fish tank in his office this time. Inside it was the biggest, ugliest, hairiest spider I'd ever seen: huge, brown, and hideous.

"Has that always been there?" I asked, pointing at the tank.

"Rocky? No! Rocky belongs to my son, David. He's in Naples with his mom this weekend. So I get to take care of Rocky. He's big, isn't he? Tarantula, from Peru. Well, let me write out this refill for you. Remember to take these regularly, Regina. They will help bring you a little clarity and . . ."

I wasn't listening anymore because I heard the flutter of millions of bat wings, thick in my ears.

"Here," he said handing me the prescription. "I'll put you down for next week?" he asked.

The sound got louder as he handed me the prescription. Suddenly, I realized the bats were symbolic of the pills. The pills were messing with my mind. I heard the voices tell me, *"Never lean on your own cognizance. Always rely on God for The Truth."*

"Uh . . . no. I think I figured this out," I said, handing the slip of paper with the prescription back. "I think I know what's wrong with me."

"Good," said Dr. Skimmer, now coldly. "Bye-bye now. I'm here if you have anything else you want to discuss. You can pay Monique at the front."

It took me three weeks to clear my head of the medication that had been messing with my visions and predictions. After my head got clear, I asked Christina to come back, so I could give her a fresh reading free.

When she came back to see me, she was four months pregnant, pissed off, and suspicious.

"Hi, Christina! I'm so sorry about what happened. I should tell you, I went on some medication to help me get through a rough time, but I now know, that the meds actually screwed up my gift."

"Right. Okay, so like, what's going to happen to me now? You tell me I win the lottery but then I actually lose my house in a fire?"

"No, God forbid! No! I need you to concentrate, Christina! Please, try to."

"Okay. Fine."

"Alright. I see someone at an old job has slandered your name," I said.

"You're sure?" Christina asked.

"Yep. Someone at the job you had before this very last one. It's taken them six months to reach everybody. This person is a woman—a tall, thin, Hispanic woman. She is also a model. Am I right?" I said.

"Yes! We got in a fight. I took her job a long time ago!" she said.

"You clearly need an image renewal," I told her.

She sighed with relief. "Okay, what's an image renewal."

"An image renewal renews the spirit so the person can stand on their own again. They can feel safe and have self-esteem. There are many ways to do one. In your case, you've experienced a lot of negative self-image situations. This has brought your energy very low. You need to renew yourself. It's very easy. Usually I charge ten thousand dollars, but I'm not going to charge you. You just pay for some new clothes. What you have is the beginnings of a curse. The mildest form of *mal occhio,* the evil eye. If you catch it in time, there should be no problem."

"Okay, okay. That sounds like something I can handle."

"And Christina, honey, I see something that I never saw before. You need to eat, honey. I know what you're doing! You must stop starving yourself and fix your eating disorder," I said.

"Wait . . . how did you know I had one of those?" she whispered.

"Christina! I mean it! I just saw it. I never saw it before, or I would have told you to get help for it earlier, before you got pregnant. That will destroy your baby and your career; this is only a pause. You will be refreshed and look wonderful. You will go and get jobs on your own. Jobs that require a pregnant model. You will restore your connections, and you will make it! I saw a split reading, Christina. One path holds wealth, stability, and a new relationship with a good man. The other holds terrible sickness. You will lose the man, the baby, and the jobs if you get sick. Right now you're just too skinny. I saw a hospital in my vision, Christina. You need to get help for your eating disorder now."

"Okay, so what do I do about the image renewal?"

"Well, in your case, you should go to Saks. I want you to get a new credit card from Saks, a brand new card. With it, I want you to purchase a whole new outfit, from head to toe: stockings, shoes, underwear, bra, outfit, accessories, all of it. Then I want you to bring it to me. I will pray over it, do a blessing over it, and burn a candle with a piece of your old clothes. You take it home and take a special bath that I'll give you. After the bath, you put on the whole outfit and burn another candle, which I will also give you. I will also ask that you recite a special prayer asking for forgiveness, mercy, and protection from God."

"And does it work right away?" Christina asked.

"Yes. Yes it does. But you must get help for the eating disorder from a licensed therapist! Please promise me. You're very young and beautiful! But you had a split reading. This could go either way. And you should make every effort to avoid illness," I warned her.

"Thanks, Regina. Thanks for helping me!!" She left upbeat and hopeful.

I didn't hear from her for a few more months. Then I got a call one morning from Christina, and she sounded depressed.

"Hi, Regina. It's me. I can't do it! I feel so ugly. I can't get out of bed. I hate being pregnant."

"It's because you're pregnant that you feel irritable. Christina, don't worry about that stuff right now. You have to get yourself better. Did you contact a therapist for the anorexia?" I asked.

"No," she said, crying.

"Listen to me! You must get up and get the clothes, or I cannot help you! Please Christina! Please, don't sink away! You have nothing to be depressed about; this is just a small blip on the screen of your life! Believe me, I see wonderful things for you!" I said, and meaning every word.

"Okay. I'll do it."

Then I didn't hear from her for three days. Now mind you, I didn't know where she lived, or I would have checked on her. I was worried sick, especially about the baby. I knew she was emotional, but she was taking it too far. So I gave her a call.

"Hello?" She answered on the phone on the very last ring.

"Christina, where do you live?" I asked.

"Why?" she asked without much energy.

"Just tell me where you live!"

"I live on the beach, on Lenox. 1215 Lenox. A little, teeny clump of houses behind Alton Road. In a blue house. Why?"

"Okay, I'm coming right over."

I drove to her house, forced her out of bed, and threw her in the shower. I put her in my car and off we went to Bal Harbour. She purchased a beautiful outfit from the sportswear department at Saks. I called them "running-around" suits—black velour with green piping and a black sporty watch from Invicta.

Though she drove me crazy the whole morning—whimpering and whining—I knew I did some good by mothering her. This beautiful woman, young and kind of healthy, with no grip, broke my heart. Her eyes were so needy and vulnerable under those platinum bangs. She was so thin by now she looked like an albino Sudanese refugee, with a huge, protruding belly from malnutrition.

We finished shopping and came back to the office where I prepared the clothing. Then I sent her off to do her thing at home, while I did my thing at the office. The next morning she called me and said she was ready to go look for work.

"I feel better, Regina! I really do!"

"Good! Good! Now remember what I told you; don't forget therapy for the starvation!"

"I won't! I'll call you back; I'm going to look for work with an old contact. I'm wearing the clothes, and I took my bath! Thank you so much, Regina! Thanks for piecing me back together!"

"Great! Good luck!" I said.

Just a few hours later she called and told me she got several go-sees and a booking for a children's catalogue. She reportedly got a booking for Pollo Tropical a week later, and several more, from Sedanos and Burdines, were quickly coming in. More of her old friends were asking her to go out. She kept calling to thank me and tell me the good news, but didn't mention an eating disorder therapist.

"Christina, I'm so happy for you! I knew an image renewal was what you needed, but I still want you to get some help for that other thing."

"Well, Regina, I'm really waiting to have this baby. I'll go after the baby's born," she said.

I prayed for her. I knew I was not the one who had been chosen to help this woman, and I left her at God's feet. I prayed for God to touch her in a mighty way—to cure her. A couple days later, she was in the hospital for anorexia. She called me from Jackson Memorial and asked me for help. I felt that the baby inside her was fine, just a little underweight.

"Honey, I can only tell you what I saw, and I told you, you needed to fix the other thing. You can beat this, too. But you'll have to start from scratch again. Are you willing to do this?"

"Yes, Regina. Thanks. Thanks for calling me back and returning my money. Thanks for nagging me to get help. Please Regina, can you see if the baby is going to be okay?!"

"She is, Christina. She is. Just get better. The baby is fine. You get better. Take care of that baby!! Call me when you need me."

Then someone, or rather *something*, made these very words spill from my mouth.

"And Christina, she will be your best friend."

That night was the first time I *ever* prayed God would deliver me from this lifestyle. I knew I could never stop *being* psychic, but I wanted to stop doing readings so badly. I prayed the mightiest prayer for myself and my family that God would deliver us from this chaos. That I would gain full recovery of my gift and not fear changing my life at this time. Most of all I prayed I would have the courage to overcome the opposition I would encounter while leaving the life.

SEVENTEEN

Shadow

S outh Beach, which used to be a home for retirees, drug addicts, and prostitutes, became a fashionable place to work and play during the mid-nineties. I capitalized on the foot traffic, working out of an office/apartment on trendy Ocean Drive, near the infamous site where Versace was later shot and killed. I also had a grand following because of a radio show I had once a week, on personal growth. Life seemed peaceful.

I occasionally got calls on my show from a particular man. He was Scottish. Here on a green card, he worked on the cruise ships and jumped from boat to boat. He'd been listening to me for three months offshore. He said I had a voice like a bird, that my voice stayed inside him, and re-played itself constantly. He was embarrassed when he called me because of his accent. He was afraid people would recognize him.

"Yuurr like the siren of the sea," he teased. "A voice so lovely it drove men to . . ." he trailed off and chuckled. "It's so sweet, so beautiful that it comforts me, when you sign off the air with, 'God bless you and may all of you have a blessed day,' while I'm at sea. 'Cause I know you really mean it."

He sounded just like Fat Bastard from *Austin Powers*, but I didn't mind—yet. It was flattering even in the Fat Bastard voice. He was very kind, not dirty or nasty. Some guys used to call and say, "Oh baby, your voice is so hot," but he was courteous.

One day, this Scot called my office. "Hello. My name is Malcolm. I really want to do a session with ya, and I dun't know why I waited so long. Maybe I'm afraid of hearing the truth about myself."

I said, "Do not fear the truth. It says in the Bible the truth shall set you free."

He asked if he could have a private session with me. I said, "Sure. I have an office on South Beach, down on Ocean Drive." He decided to come in the next day.

That night after feeding the kids, I looked at the list of all the people who had appointments the next day, and I did an energy test. This consists of burning a candle and calling on my higher power to show me who needs me the most the next day. The candle flickers and the shadow of the flame gets very dark closest to the name of the one who will drain me the most. It was definitely Malcolm. I felt sorry for him.

He came shuffling down the street on Monday afternoon—beefy, sweaty, and red as a lobster, but very polite.

"Good afternoon, Regina. It's a real pleasure to meet you after all this time," he said.

"Likewise, Malcolm. What I need from you is a key chain, some change—something you've had in your pocket for a while, something metal of no value, but that's been with you. Your name and date of birth. Then give me five hundred dollars wrapped in a piece of paper. On the paper write down three good things you want me to make happen for you this year." The money part always makes people a little tense, so I added the wishes bit to help them relax.

I looked at his handwriting and a little metal guardian angel he'd had on his key chain. Those objects connected me instantly, and I knew there were antidepressants, major issues with depression, and sexual abuse as a child. I knew he was battling something. He handed his crumpled bills to me with a crooked little smile, hopeful and eager. I smiled back, nervously. His three wishes were to fall in love, to have a woman to love him for rest of his life, and to be successful.

I told him, "I see sexual abuse when you were a child."

Tears welled in his eyes and rolled down his cheeks. He said, "How

do you see these things? I just don't know how you know these things!"
Mind you, he'd been listening to my show for three months.

"I see you've been having a lot of problems with love. And you
haven't had a good relationship. I do see a woman with short, dark hair.
She's tall, slender, and attractive. Who is she?"

"Oh! That's Rosario," he said. "She's a friend from the cruise ship. I
just met her through mutual friends," he said, clasping his stubby fingers
together in his lap.

"You really like her," I said.

"Does she like *me*?"

"The cards show she does like you, and she thinks you're a kind person," I said.

"That makes me happy!" he said. Rosario genuinely *did* like him as a
person. She thought he was considerate, kind, generous, and funny.

I continued, "But either she's coming out of or is about to come out
of a relationship where she's been abused. She has issues with men."

Suddenly, I saw the madness in his household while he was just a kid.
His father was an alcoholic, and his father's friends sexually abused him.

I said, "Malcolm, you've been very confused about yourself; you've
had many issues with yourself."

"Yes."

"The confusion is about your sexuality."

"Yes! Yes!" But he wasn't willing to talk about it. He never once said,
"Yeah, I thought I was gay at one time," or "Yeah, I think I may be bisex-
ual." When you read for people, sometimes you get a feeling you
shouldn't open Pandora's box.

Sex abuse is the worst thing that can happen to a child. It's as if your
parents put you out in the world, at whatever age the abuse began, without schooling, without housing, and told you to make your own way. Children aren't meant for sex. It robs them of childhood. It makes them
shattered adults in tiny bodies and leaves the child that was once there, a
tiny, empty corpse.

I saw he had a good reputation and a good name at his job on the cruise line. He was a ship's steward. He didn't have problems making money. He lived simply and invested his money in Cayman Island commercial real estate.

At the end of the reading, he said, "My God! You are the sweetest woman on this world. I just love listening to your voice. It soothes me."

I said, "I think you're a very nice person, too, Malcolm. Good luck. If there's anything I can do for you, don't hesitate to come by or call me."

He stood up, gripped my hand like a vise as he shook it. I shrugged it off as a "Scottish" thing. Two weekends later, he said he wanted to come by to speak to me.

"Regina! I have a date with Rosario!"

"Great! I'm so happy for you."

He arrived in the same army jacket and jeans and had the same vise-grip handshake. He kept saying how much he wanted a good woman in his life. He asked me how many children I had, but I didn't tell him. He still said I had very strong maternal qualities.

Then he asked, "Where are you from?"

"I'm from Romania," I lied.

"No wonder you are so beautiful. You sound so beautiful. Your hair is so beautiful, so beautiful," he said reaching out to touch a lock of hair, next to my cheek. I quickly pulled back.

"Oh come on!" I said. "We don't have time for that. I have to go into my next reading; she's already here. And you, my friend, have a date with Rosario!"

"Well, I want another reading with you—tomorrow, after the date."

"It's too soon. Give it at least a month."

A lot of people balk when I tell them I can only give them readings every three months because they want weekly, daily, or hourly readings. But that defeats the purpose of having faith in God, wanting to turn your life over to God's will. God knows what is in every person's heart. Malcolm called me after the date anyway, and I did the session for him out of pity that afternoon. As I was looking around, I did see she was slightly attracted to him, but I saw a big problem.

"Malcolm, I definitely like her energy, and you have good chemistry, but you both have major issues with the opposite sex. I'm going to do a meditation on her. Bring me her picture, if you have one.

"I'll be back next week," he said, chipper.

Sure enough, next Sunday came and he dropped off a piece of paper with her date of birth and a small photo. That night, I discovered through the meditation Rosario was a lesbian, and that Malcolm had a guy he would see once in a while. They were dating each other while having sex with same-sex partners. I called him immediately.

"Malcolm, how come I see a younger man in your life?"

"I don't quite understand you."

"I see a younger guy in your life."

He said, "Oh yes. I know who that is. That's Kevin. He was my flat-mate."

I didn't understand what a flatmate was, so I repeated it, "Who is Kevin?"

"My cabinmate." Then he admitted he'd been having sex with Kevin because he'd been confused and that he thought I already knew about it. But he did not elaborate.

"Does this mean I'm gay?" he asked after a few moments of silence.

"It means you're having problems because of your past and what was done to you. You're so confused."

"I just feel like I can't, I mean, I will never have a good woman. I call Kevin but it doesn't make me feel any better, it just makes me feel worse. It breaks me heart that God does not want me to be with a good woman. And, I dun' know, what does this mean?"

"Malcolm, God is not punishing you. It means you're not gay."

"Oh thank you so much Regina! I knew you would figure it out. I knew you were the one to help me."

I said, "Malcolm, Rosario has had experiences with women, too. She's been having an affair with a woman off and on, and the woman is married. The husband does not know. They were lovers in college."

"Oh God! I need help. I need help to take this confusion away."

Visions of drunken men coming over to Malcolm's house came over me. They got his father drunk and were grabbing at Malcolm, raping him and trying to choke him. Finally, I saw a red Jeep.

I said, "Listen, Malcolm, you honestly need help. I am going to do the other part of the meditation to see what I can do to help you."

"I'll do anything you tell me. If you tell me to stand outside naked in the rain, I'll stand outside naked in the rain."

We both started chuckling. Then I said, "I also see a lot of medication around you, sweetie; what is this? I see antidepressants and sleeping pills, and I also see that last holiday season you were not well at all."

"No. I tried to commit suicide. I wanted to kill myself."

Poor Malcolm. The only woman he had liked in so long was definitely gay. But I didn't see he was gay—not at all. So I sent him lots of herbs to take baths in while he was at sea. I sent him some psalms for meditation to clear his soul and ask forgiveness for what he did with Kevin because it did not come from his heart. I told him to ask God to help him find forgiveness in his heart for his father.

Two months into his healing, he was feeling better. He would always tell me I was such a beautiful person and that he loved me. Whenever we finished out sessions, he'd send me a thank-you card and flowers. My youngest boy was very little at the time, and sometimes, if I was home when he called, he'd hear him playing or chattering in the background.

He would say, "I hear the little wee man in the background. He must be beautiful like you. I never knew you were married."

"You never asked."

Each time he would sign off with, "I love you! I love you! I love you!" I would say, "Thank you, Malcolm." I never said "I love you" back.

I worked for him for about six months, on his days ashore. He stopped dating Rosario because he knew it was a dead-end situation. He stopped seeing Kevin. He stopped wondering if he would ever be happy because he started to focus on his healing.

We were almost done. Once a client is done and on the path to full recovery, I make my exit. I don't stick around because I'm not hired to be a companion. The rest is supposed to be between that person and God. But they never want to let me go. Malcolm was no exception. I would get weekly money from him, as if I was "on retainer." He would call me all the time, from port, wherever he docked.

Then one afternoon, around his birthday, he called and said, "I'm so lonely—I wish I had someone to cook for. Do you like home-cooked meals?"

I said, "Yes, of course I do."

"I bet you have a man that loves you very much. I bet your man is always around you because you're so beautiful. I bet he never leaves you alone. How long have you been married?"

"A long time, Malcolm," I said.

"I wonder what it would be like to be married to you for a long time? I wonder what it would be like to always have you there—to see you every morning and every night, smell your perfume, touch your hair."

"Malcolm, are you okay?"

"No, I'm not okay! I want to be around a woman like you! Tell me why can't I have a woman like you. You're the psychic!!"

I said, "Sweetie, come on! You're just lonely. I'm the closest thing you have to a girlfriend, but I told you from the beginning I am not, nor could I ever be."

But he wasn't listening. "Why don't you ever say you love me?! You *never* say you love me!"

"Malcolm, you need to continue this treatment with a psychologist. I weaned you off Kevin and helped you through Rosario. I taught you to pray and meditate the rancor and shame from your soul. But now you are trying to make me feel guilty. You know I am not now, nor ever was, a love interest, Malcolm."

"*No!* I don't want to see a psychologist. I want a picture of you. Can't I please have a picture of you?"

"I don't look good in pictures," I said.

"I just want a picture of my best friend!"

Now my guides were telling me not to feel compassion but to be careful. So again, I decided it was time to pull away. Up until now, I had made accommodations to counsel him. If I was watching a movie or eating dinner with my kids, I would go out to the beach to talk to him on the phone. Sometimes I would even meet him at the office because he would get upset if my baby was cooing in the background.

Well, a few nights later, I had a dream. It was no ordinary dream; it was much more serious than that. When a psychic connects with a client, that client also connects with the psychic, and visually speaking, the two can communicate without using words. So too can they be with each other, right next to each other, in the same room or situation, by leaving their bodies spiritually.

That night I awoke inside the red Jeep—the very same one I'd been having visions about. I was in the driver's seat, hands on the steering wheel. I felt somebody looking at me. I turned my head toward the passenger seat, and there was Malcolm! He was sitting right next to me, grinning. I can still see that elflike face. He was staring at me with piercing blue eyes and that weird, long, pointy nose. He had the surplus army jacket on, and I remember he kept on grinning and grinning. Then all the car doors locked by themselves, and I couldn't get away. I kept asking, "Malcolm, is that you?? Is that you??" And he just sat there, grinning. I grew hysterical trying to get out—to flee that beefy face. I was crying, sobbing, and begging him to let me go! But the man wouldn't talk! He put his fingers on his lips like "shhhhh!!"

I woke up in cold sweat. I was the victim of what psychics call a "psychic kidnapping." My angels speak to me in dreams or visions and prayers, and now, just like when I was young, they used the same urgency to tell me to let go of Malcolm. I rolled over and screamed. I knew Malcolm spiritually summoned me from my bed that night and terrorized me in that red Jeep.

The next weekend was Easter. My grandmother, the kids, and I were going to church services and, later, an Easter egg hunt. We were at the service when I got a call on my cell phone from Malcolm. I wouldn't answer. He left me a message that unless I called him back in twenty minutes, he would commit suicide and leave a note that it was my fault.

Sometimes, psychics go through psychological warfare similar to the cycle of abuse that battered women endure: threats, manipulation through guilt, terror, and on rare occasions, actual physical abuse. I read about a psychic who had a client whom she counseled through a divorce. She predicted he would have to give up the house and the child because of his violent manner. He did, in the end. Throughout, she counseled him, prayed for his inner peace, and begged him to seek professional help for his anger. Each time he wanted a reading, he would call crying that he would commit suicide should she refuse. One night, he came to her for what she thought was another reading. But instead, he cut off her head and placed it in the window of her little storefront. Her children found it the next day when they came to look for her. That's a true story. It happened in California.

I concentrated all my prayers that he would not commit suicide and would soon be on his way. Then I dialed his number.

"Hello," I said.

"Are you having a lovely day with your sons?" he asked.

"Malcolm, you can't leave threatening messages anymore."

"No, no . . . I'm going to sit here praying I meet a wonderful woman like you," he said.

"Praying is good way to spend the day," I said.

"You really are that innocent, aren't you?"

"Malcolm, try to focus on your accomplishments and not dwell on the past. Make a new life resolution on this day. It's Easter. Give one day a month to a charity and offer it for an end to your loneliness," I encouraged him.

"You always make me feel so good! When I'm in the dumps you take me out," he said.

I told him, "You have natural spring. You're meant to bounce back. Stop feeling like a victim because you're not a victim!"

"I'm so blessed to have found you!! I . . . I love you." He started to whimper. Then he got quiet.

I said, "You know what? I care about your life, too."

All of a sudden, the hairs on my neck stood on end and the top of my scalp stung. I felt uncomfortable, like I forgot something. Then I got an uneasy feeling like somebody was putting their fists in my stomach and churning it.

The church service ended, and we made our way toward the front doors. The mass of people were squished together. As I walked through the doorway, someone just grazed my back with their hand. It felt so cold, though it was hot that day. I reeled around. I looked between people's heads, but I couldn't see anyone who looked like they may have done it. Malcolm was always in the back of my mind, with his "I love you" and "I want a woman like you" going round and round in my head. Completely distracted, I pushed the stroller over to the car. On my windshield were the most beautiful red roses. They made chills run up my arms. I froze.

"What are these? Who the hell left me flowers?" I growled.

My grandmother made the sign of the cross. No letter, no nothing. I looked around and saw nothing unusual, just people getting into their cars. My body started shaking uncontrollably, and I don't even remember strapping the kids in the car because it had just dawned on me that when he said he was "praying for a woman like me," he was doing it in the *same church*.

The things that kept coming into my mind were the red Jeep; the dream; the army jacket; the beefy face; stubby fingers; vise-grip; long, pointy nose; and the roses. Everything was revolving through my brain over and over again, like a maddening carousel.

I've heard stories about Gypsies in Germany who were hunted like wild game. I remembered a story I heard my great-grandma once told about how German nobles use to shoot Gypsy mothers and their suckling babes, to use their heads as trophies. I felt hunted. I ripped the roses off my car and placed them on the ground, then drove off, finally accepting he'd been following me—probably for some time now.

At 3:00 A.M. I was awakened by a private call. "I want to tell you how lovely you are. You are a lovely, lovely wom . . . er . . . I mean lady. And I love you, beautiful."

"Malcolm, are you drinking?" I whispered. "Malcolm, where are you?"

"Why?"

"Well, I got some roses on my car today. Do you know anything about that?"

"Why did you throw them on the ground??!!"

Then he told me I was beautiful again and hung up. I checked all my doors, making sure they were locked.

The next day, I woke up around nine. I tried to go about my daily routine: banking, bills, groceries, the kids, the house, my reading schedule. Inside, I was telling myself, *I am not going to worry about Malcolm. I am not going to freak out.* But I felt unsettled. The phone rang.

"Hello Malcolm."

"Thank God! I thought you abandoned me!" It hadn't even been twenty-four hours since we last spoke. "So have you meditated on me today, Regina?" he asked.

"No, Malcolm. I haven't had a chance, and I'm booked solid at the office today. Can you please call me later today?"

"Right. Later on then?"

"Yes, Malcolm."

"You're going to answer, right? No tricks?"

"Malcolm, have I ever played a trick on you?"

"No, but I've been meditating on you, and I see you're going to try to trick me."

"Malcolm, are you playing psychic with me?"

"I'll call you later, at the office."

I suspected that, by now, he knew my schedule and my habits. Maybe he would try to rape me or kill me. But I knew my guides would not allow that. I became exhausted thinking about Malcolm and his whereabouts. So I canceled my appointments, debating whether or not I should go to the police.

I forced myself to go grocery shopping. I left the baby and my grandmother at home. As I was putting the groceries in the trunk, what do I see on the windshield of my Rover? A single red rose. I started crying. My cell phone rang. "Hello?" I said.

"I've seen you in my meditation. You're wearing a white flowing skirt with a blue T-shirt and white sandals."

"Malcolm, stop! You aren't meditating! You left another rose on my windshield! What's the matter with you? Have you been fired? How is it you are still in Miami?"

"I've been seeing you in my meditation. Were you driving in some sort of an SUV? I saw it in meditation that you have two boys."

I said, "Look! I've had enough! I know you did not see any of this in meditation. I don't know what kind of game you're playing or who you think you're playing it with, but you've crossed the line of friendship! You've crossed the line of client! What do want from me?"

"Regina, why are you screaming at me? I thought you would love the rose."

I began looking around the parking lot, checking inside cars and around dumpsters.

"I have to speak to you. Your voice comforts me," he said.

I carefully took the rose off the windshield, put it on the ground, and drove away. That rocked his little world. I got a call in the car, again.

"I want to know, *why did you throw the rose on the floor?* Is that what I mean to you? Is that what you do to your friends?"

"Where are you?" I growled.

"I'm driving." He said, pleased with himself.

"*Where are you physically, Malcolm?*! I'm going to call the police and tell them that you're stalking me, you bastard! That you threatened to commit suicide, and that you aim to make me the responsible party!"

"I can't hear you very well. I'll call you back."

I looked in my rearview mirror. There were so many cars behind me; where was the red Jeep? Should I go home or call the police? What would I possibly say? Please, dear God! I was so scared. I felt he would take me away, and I'd never see my kids again!

That afternoon, I put a private eye on him. He had been around the corner on South Beach in a hotel the whole time! He had gone on leave from the cruise ships about one month back and had been watching my every move. In a bold action, I went against the *Baro* and filed a restraining order against him the very next day. I figured I'd already broken all the rules—kicked my husband out of the house, claimed my children, wore *gaje* fashions, and was a career woman who just *happened* to be Rom. Safety seemed to be a reasonable cause for breaking away from strict Rom dicta.

Nonetheless, Malcolm kept calling, leaving messages that said, "I miss you, and I love you. I get so upset when you talk to other men at the office." Finally, after I sent my kids and grandmother to stay in New York, I dialed his number.

"The time has come for me to tell you I feel uncomfortable, Malcolm. I am a spiritual woman of God, and a married woman, and your actions and statements make me feel uncomfortable."

He laughed a wicked laugh.

"Look, I'm not gonna hurt you, darlin'. I just want to talk to you. I think you're beautiful. I think you're so beautiful. I see us together. I know what I can do for you. I know how I can make you feel."

I said, "I want you to talk to my husband."

"I would like that. I'd like to tell him he's a lucky man."

I put Malcolm on hold and dialed Romy at his brother's house. Up until now, he had been completely unaware of how out-of-control the situation had become. He called Malcolm and said, "Look buddy, I know you have some issues and problems, but you have to understand, *my wife is the single most important thing to me. She is the eyes in my head.* Do you understand that Malcolm?! You're gonna see me up close and personal, if you don't stop. So go about your vacation and leave my wife alone!"

Romy said, "G, lemme come over! I need to protect you! You see, G?! You think you can be alone and without me?! You need protection." But I refused to let him come over.

The next day I get the biggest arrangement of flowers and a card. I thought it was Romy, but the card read, "I'm sorry. I cried all night last night. I'm leaving on the next ship. I promise I did not come into town to hurt you."

Three weeks went by peacefully, and my uncomfortable feeling went away. My scalp stopped burning, and I stopped having visions of the red Jeep. One day I arrived at my house after grocery shopping. The house phone rang—a private call.

"Hi," said Malcolm.

"Hi."

"Can I just have five minutes of your time?" he asked, innocently.

I have no idea what I was thinking, but of course, I gave him five minutes.

"I met someone. She's warm and nurturing. Just like you," Malcolm told me.

"Good, Malcolm. I want you to be happy. I want you at peace."

"I am going to be with her soon. I just called to say good-bye."

"Okay, Malcolm, good-bye, and God bless."

He hung up. I put away the groceries. I walked down the long hallway to my bedroom to change, and the room had been ransacked! Pillows were torn up and littered the floor, drawers were yanked out, and contents spilled. The window sash was wide open. Family photographs, my underwear, and a crucifix were missing!

I called Romy, who'd been sick with the flu.

"Romy! Romy! God Almighty! Malcolm's been here. He trashed our room! And listen to what he took, the bastard! He took my underwear and our family pictures. Oh my God!"

"I'm on my way, G!" Romy assured me.

I ran outside the house and waited for Romy, who arrived in fifteen minutes.

Then it all happened so fast. As Romy was checking under our bed, the nutcase stuck out his grubby hand from underneath and grabbed

Romy's shirt collar, pulling him down. I started screaming. Romy started punching.

"Why, Malcolm? What did I do to you? I never led you on! *Why, Malcolm?!*"

He didn't have a chance to answer. With the help of my brothers, Romy dumped Malcolm, bloody and smashed, in the underpass at Haulover Beach. Malcolm was seen back on a cruise ship about two months later, I heard from a close Gypsy source, who worked at the Port.

The entire psychic industry caters to the obsession of ordinary people wanting to obtain "something." Unfortunately, for Malcolm, trading money to acquire a Gypsy psychic lover was not in the cards.

EIGHTEEN

A Tale of Two Psychics

That night, when Romy went back to his brother's house, I thought about him. I missed him. Of all the people I'd ever known in my life, he'd been my only best friend, my confidante, my *lumnia*.

I was about to call him when my cell phone rang. I'd had all the calls forwarded from my office, and I was not in the mood to see another psycho model so soon. I let the message service pick up. As soon as the person was done, I picked up the message.

The person's voice sounded very friendly. The message said, "Hi, this is Yvonne Carey for *The Miami Herald*. I am calling to speak to the Miami psychic. I do new business stories in this zone, and I'd like to do a story on yours. Please return my call if, you are, indeed, the Miami psychic."

I don't do reporters, particularly ones that seek me out, but for some reason, I had a tugging in my heart that I needed to talk to her. I called her back and introduced myself.

"Hi, Regina. How are you?" she said.

"I'm fine, thank you, but explain this 'story' thing to me."

"I want to come and do a 'new business' story on you and take your photograph. People need to know what you're about. It would probably bring in a lot of business," she said.

"Yes, I'm sure it would bring in business. I'm not sure I want it. And I don't do photos."

"That's okay. No worries. We can just take a picture of the cards and the office. Would you be okay with that?"

"By the way, how much do you charge for a reading? I'd like to come see you. I love psychics. I'm a believer. My mom passed away in May of '97, and I saw her immediately afterward. She predicted the birth of my eldest son."

I felt something positive in her words.

"Well, come in, and we'll talk," I said. "Tomorrow I could open up the office for you. We could do the interview there."

While I slept that night, I dreamt that I was standing on a slate patio surrounding a lushly landscaped pool, behind a beautiful ranch-style house, on a cliff, overlooking the Pacific Ocean. I also saw a petite brunette inside my Jacuzzi, with a margarita in her hand, flashing a brilliant smile. I awoke earlier than usual the next morning and primped for the interview. I was wondering what she would ask me, and I hoped no one would come into the office. I kissed the kids good-bye and got into my Bentley.

The day was another gloriously beautiful South Florida day, with a blazing bright sun and an ocean breeze swaying the palms along the causeway. I felt lighter than usual and decided to make a special effort to greet this woman the way I used to greet my clients—*warmly*.

I peeked out the window and knew who she was before she even came in. She emerged from a gold Volvo, on time and dressed in a khaki suit. She looked like the woman in my dream. I shook her hand.

"Hi! I'm Regina. Thanks for coming. Why don't we go inside the office, and we can talk."

"Thanks for letting me come! I'm Yvonne. I'll only take twenty minutes of your time. I promise my interviews are painless," she said sweetly.

"So, when did you know you were psychic?" she began. I found it interesting that she did not ask me *if* I was psychic or *how* I knew that I was psychic. I told her my story about the near-death experience, growing into my powers, and what sorts of work I could do, when I got a bad feeling. But the feeling wasn't about Yvonne. It was about something inside a closet in her house.

"After we're done here, I'll do a free reading for you."

"Actually, I'm not allowed to accept a free reading. I'll pay for it. You know what they say, 'Leave only footprints and take only photographs.'"

"Oh, okay. But I just need to tell you one thing."

"Hold on! Let me pay you. Here," she said, handing me one hundred dollars. "Is this enough for a half hour?" She seemed familiar enough with our prices.

"It's just one little thing: the shoebox in your closet. You have to get rid of the shoe box in your bedroom closet. Get rid of it. Your husband will find the things you have hidden in it. Take the box, put it in a garbage bag, and throw it away in another city."

"Oh my God. Okay, I will! Thanks!"

Later that week the reporter called and said that her air conditioning had leaked inside her bedroom closet. The repairman and her husband had been in there trying to fix the leak, and when they left, her clothes and shoe boxes had been turned over and scattered around the closet floor. She said that inside the box were all her secret feelings, some diaries she'd been keeping about how miserable she had been in her marriage for years. They told how desparately she wanted a divorce and how she was slowly setting aside money to get one. She was so grateful, she told me if I ever wanted to get out of this business, to give her a call, and we'd write a book about my career and my clients.

God answered my prayers that afternoon. Yvonne brought a partnership agreement contract to my house, and we signed it together. The same evening I went for a ride, and while I was on the road, I called Romy.

"Meet me at Carpaccio's in Bal Harbour in a couple of hours."

"Anywhere! Thank you so much!! I'm so sorry, G! I'm going to be better to you and the kids! I swear in the name of Jesus! I swear on the Bible! I swear on my mother's grave! I swear on . . ."

"Stop swearing, numbnuts!" I said, giggling.

"I will! I will! I'm sorry! It's just that I . . ."

"Just meet me in a couple of hours." I hung up, relieved and hopeful. I wondered if Romy would be able to get past my news. I prayed for us, silently, begging God to have mercy on us both and to do His will in my household. The truth was, I hadn't had peace since I began taking on the nefarious, big-money clients. Whatever Brooklyn may have been, with the taunting, the jeering, and the accusations . . . it was my home. I had allowed myself to be kicked out of my home, so to speak, by other people's opinions. They were what had mattered most, not God's opinion.

However, lately, the presence of God hung over me like a floodlight. I'd used the gift God gave me to try to help people, but never really turned any soul over to God, which was a *bezake*. God did not mind that I was wealthy, influential, or successful. God never condemns wealth or status, as long as you use it to give glory to Him. From the beginning, I skillfully neglected turning any of my clients completely over to my creator. A parade of opportunities to steer clients in the right direction strutted before my eyes while I waited for Romy, and with it, the harsh reality that I had failed in my one mission.

I was so distracted, I never even saw him until he sat down. He looked like I had placed a curse on him. His hair, or whatever was left of it, was stark white. His skin was pale and wrinkled. His clothes hung off his bony body like a wet sack. He'd probably dropped fifty pounds. I felt so bad.

"I think you've had enough," I said.

"What are you saying, G?"

"Romy, no one can punish us worse than ourselves. If God can forgive us, then I forgive you," I said. Romy started to tear up. "More importantly, I'm going to leave my mistakes on the cross." I explained to him how I knew that debauchery and stagnation had taken over our lives. We took our good fortune for granted, which had led to our problems. I told him that I understood his general lack of fulfillment led to false love or infatuation. I believed I became intoxicated with my ability to gain people's trust, and it had resulted in arrogance and dangerous overconfidence.

The time of prosperity and profit from "a card table and a sign" was officially *over*. I illustrated how, if we were to have success and generosity in material things again, our power and influence had to be turned to nobler pursuits. Philanthropy was the balance of physical and spiritual life, and we could not be diverted from the right path a second time. The voice of duty and honor was calling me. This is was the *science* of my undertaking.

Romy's eyes glowed with appreciation. "I will never hurt you again as long as I live," he declared.

"Oh, I know you won't, Romy." I saw it in him. I felt his guilt. I felt his pain and the shame. But he wasn't alone. I knew in my soul the blame and the shame was shared by us both. You don't give in to becoming a greedy, manipulative, bitchy psychic and expect your spouse not to change into a lecherous, predatory escape artist.

He begged me to continue. I told him God was the only justified source of power. Blind faith in Gypsy tradition and psychic abilities was the old school—now outdated and useless for me. I assured him that he had always been supportive, sympathetic, and loyal. But lately, I'd been systematically receiving instructions and guidance with more clarity than ever before, and I had heard my higher, inner voice. I *got it*.

I said, "Romy, the time has come for us to part as husband and wife and to continue on our right and true spiritual paths."

His jaw dropped. The waiter poured him a large glass of water.

"As a human being, I won't be able to stop punishing you for this. For all the pain we've caused each other. But as a friend, I've never needed you more in my life to help me complete the task of raising our children and straightening out this psychic *mess*. Please don't leave me. But grant me a *gaje* divorce."

"G, you know I can't do that! Don't ask me to do anything the *gaje* way except pray and dress like them! You don't know what you're saying! Maybe you just need to take a trip and be alone for a while," Romy said.

"No, Romy. I need my life back, to start over and do the right thing by my children, and my maker, and myself. Staying together would indicate a successful marriage, but it would be an utterly unfulfilling conclusion. We'd be on the same, dismal track: satisfaction from comfort unattached to any sense of love. Let me go."

"I'll never let you go, Gina! My family paid twenty-five thousand for you! We own you. You know that. In Jesus' name, you know I can't let you go, G!"

"Romy, I don't want to do any more readings. I'm not going to do any more psychic readings. I'm going to write a book. Ever since I started this, it's been for all the wrong reasons! I thought if I charged enough, they'd stop asking. But they don't, Romy! They never do, and they never will. I can't keep taking on these fucked-up people! They're eating me alive! They're tearing the words out of my throat!

"Morning, noon, and night these people call me and beg me for one spell, then two, then three, then eight!! And we still never seem to have enough money! The money! It's always the money! Why is it we never have enough money? The boys need laptops, the house needs a new roof, the psychos keep coming, and God's truth is left on the ground while we worship the almighty *gaje* dollar.

"I don't wanna do readings anymore! Do you hear me?! *I'm not going to do any more psychic readings!!!*"

"Gina, calm down! We're in public! You're crazy—this is crazy talk! What'll we live on? We got bills, G! We got kids! You know what your duty is!"

"It's not up to you what I do anymore, Romy."

"Like hell! You're my wife and my life, and I can't let you go, Gina! I . . . I love you."

"I know you do, Romy. I love you, too! But can't you see what this does to us? What it does to the children? Together we end up splitting hairs about money, status, and the Gypsies. Those details don't matter, Romy! Our faults feed off one another and create chaos! The readings are no good, Romy. God wants us to do *His* work, not ours."

"If you leave, I get everything, Gina—the house, the cars, the kids, the money. Everything!! You get nothing! I'll give you nothing!"

"That's not love, Romy. That's spite."

"Nothing G! And that's fucking final!" He got up and stomped off, leaving the bill.

Any money made by any member of the Gypsy household goes to the husband. A Gypsy woman must never speak ill of her husband and must always treat him with great respect in public, a trait which is considered to bring good fortune to the entire family. Gypsies are also fiercely territorial. I took a deep breath and looked up at the sky. At last I'd said it. It was a step, and I was thankful.

Acknowledgments

W e want to thank Judith Regan, the bewitching powerhouse that is ReganBooks, for trafficking our weird story; to our agent and mentor, the illustrious CJL, for doing a favor for his old college buddy "Chief," after not having seen him for twenty years; to "Chief," for heeding his "nagging" wife, Lynn, about helping her friend YV, who "had a book"; to Sunny, for acting as devoted referee when key players lost faith; to each other, Regina Milbourne and Yvonne Carey, for propping, bracing, and buttressing each other up through prayer, white lies, big dreams, and magic during our purge; a little shout-out to Sal, who hooked us up with our first call to the king of the *GoodFellas*; to all our dead and angels who helped us lay it down; and to all people everywhere who *believe in the power of prayer*.